AGELESS ADOBE
History and Preservation in Southwestern Architecture

AGELESS ADOBE

History and Preservation in Southwestern Architecture

Jerome Iowa

SUNSTONE PRESS

SANTA FE

Cover photograph by Carl D. Condit

Sunstone books may be purchased for educational, business, or
sales promotional use. For information please write:
Special Markets Department, Sunstone Press, P.O. Box 2321,
Santa Fe, New Mexico 87504-2321.

Library of Congress Cataloging in Publication Data

Iowa, Jerome,
    Ageless adobe:
    history and preservation in Southwestern architecture.

    Bibliography: p.
    Includes index.
    1. Building, Adobe--New Mexico--Conservation and
restoration. 2. Historic buildings--New Mexico--Conservation and
restoration. 3. Architecture and energy conservation--New Mexico.
4. Solar energy--New Mexico.
I. Title.
NA730.N38I59   1985   720'.9789   84-16337
ISBN: 0-86534-034-X

Published in 1985 by SUNSTONE PRESS
                    Post Office Box 2321
                    Santa Fe, NM 87504-2321 / USA
                    (505) 988-4418 / orders only (800) 243-5644
                    FAX (505) 988-1025

The author's research for this publication was financed in part
with federal funds from Heritage Conservation and Recreation
Service, Department of the Interior, through the Historic
Preservation Bureau, State Planning Division, Department
of Finance and Administration, State of New Mexico.

The content and opinions contained herein do not necessarily
reflect the views or policies of the Department of the Interior,
nor does the mention of trade names or commercial products
constitute endorsements or recommendations by the
Department of the Interior.

CONTENTS

ACKNOWLEDGEMENTS

The author wishes to express his appreciation to the following individuals and agencies for their assistance in the preparation of this book.

• Peter van Dresser, planner, designer, and humanist; President of the New Mexico Council for Sustainable Growth, which in many ways encouraged this project.

Peter van Dresser was buried in simple dignity at Ghost Ranch in June 1983. To his vision of regional tradition, melded with appropriate planning and technology — an idea, like its author, challenging, harmonious yet complex — this work is dedicated.

• R. David Thompson, author of many of the original illustrations, a friend and a gentleman.

• B. Nanci Caldwell, for preparation of the manuscript and, always-supportive, administrative assistance.

• Marcia Muth, Justin Estoque and Boyd Pratt, for editorial comment

• The New Mexico Office of Historic Preservation and the National Park Service, for their assistance in funding the original study. This earlier draft, obscurely and ironically titled *Learning from Las Cruces*, appeared as a very small monographic edition in 1982.

• And the numerous individuals, institutions and publishers who cooperated in the permission to reprint many of the photographs and illustrations.

The Nestor Armijo house in Las Cruces, one of the few remaining historic buildings in the downtown area, flanked in the photo by (left) the Highrise-Box and (right) the Pancake-Box, and (foreground) parking lot.

INTRODUCTION

The earliest draft of this book carried the somewhat facetious title *Learning from Las Cruces*. Hard-pressed for a title more picturesque, more romantically descriptive, the author settled on something which represented a sardonic in-joke for the architectural intellegencia. What book on architecture has ever been complete without a thorough disparaging of that which went just before? *Learning from Las Cruces* was never intended to be the title, it just happened for lack of a more interesting solution. Even that earlier text had nothing whatsoever to do with the Sunbelt city of Las Cruces, New Mexico: except as a post mortem on those features of native building wisdom — and style — which are lost, demolished or disregarded in the American quest for something new.

In fact, Las Cruces is a growing city on the southern Rio Grande, and few of its good historic structures have survived the spread of parking strips and hermetically-sealed boxes, called modern architecture.

Robert Venturi and Denise Scott-Brown's epic treatise on Late Modern architecture, *Learning from Las Vegas* (the source for our own satirical namesake) was a milestone in the highly intellectualized appreciation of the American roadside aesthetic: glorifying the symbolism of mobility, disposability, commercialism, crass allusion. Perhaps with 'informed' irony, perhaps not. The ideas of Venturi and Brown caught the imagination of many thoughtful minds in the design professions... for a time at least. Its freshness, outrageous irreverence and candid savor of buildings clearly out of the stream of 'good architecture' — "the ugly and ordinary" — made *Learning from Las Vegas* a provocative intellectual detour into the real stuff of the built American scene.

Though some of the book's ideas seem to have sunk into the conceptual vocabulary of contemporary design thought, little more than ten years later, much of *Learning from Las Vegas* is regarded as a kind of racy period piece. Why? Perhaps a growing awareness of, and revulsion toward, the dehumanization of the proliferating environmental junkshop and its shameless built-in energy cost.

In what is now being called the 'Post Modern' era, designers everywhere are turning to the roots of historicism and regionalism to find cues for meaningful structures: meaningful both in terms of basic human response to building aesthetics, and in terms of a building's ability to address, in an intelligent and conserving manner, the characteristics of context, site and climate.

The American Southwest has a rich and vital architectural history, and an extraordinary stock of good historic buildings. These seem frequently to be not great monumental edifices but smaller, regionalized structures, built on principals of native folk wisdom and tradition, often of the earth itself. Simple, direct, adobe buildings may no longer be the preponderant type, but they continue to be popular. While other areas of the country are rediscovering the ways of indigenous building, we find in the Southwest that we have lived with them all along. However, these historic buildings — particularly those of adobe — have some distinct peculiarities in both preservation and energy conservation.

The concerns of this book are principally two: first, to look at the Southwest's architectural history, with an especial eye to the particulars of New Mexico, for evident building tradition there is not only older, but less diluted by outside influence (not to mention the focus of the original Las Cruces study). Second, to consider actual ways in which old buildings of regional type — particularly those of adobe — can be preserved and rehabilitated; optimizing conservation features while not impinging upon historic character or architectural significance, or undermining their structural future.

Las Cruces, New Mexico — the easily exploited namesake of this book's original title — is not exceptional; it is like towns all across America, which have swept aside much of their historic heritage. But — as pursued in Chapter 14 — older buildings are often not only more efficient in overall energy use, but consume less energy, and cost less to rehabilitate than to tear and replace. Beyond the worthy virtue of an informative past, we discover — not too late — that old buildings have not only a certain innate charm, but they work.

Jerome Iowa
Santa Fe, 1984

PART I:
ARCHITECTURE OF THE AMERICAN SOUTHWEST: A BRIEF HISTORY

INTRODUCTION:
CULTURAL TRADITIONS IN STYLE AND TECHNOLOGY

New Mexico has an older building heritage than any other part of the United States; especially impressive is the influence ancient and historic regional styles still play in much of today's construction. Part I of this book presents a brief historic summary of changes in architectural style and building technology and some commentary on energy in the eventful chronology.

In spite of its early settlement by Europeans, New Mexico remained clearly the frontier into the early 20th century (and it could be argued that much of it is still a frontier). With its own indigenous architectural tradition and considerable remoteness, essentially non-native styles — such as Greek Revival, Victorian, even Moderne — were late in arriving here, and were disseminated only slowly throughout the territory, often in curiously mutated forms.

As a result, there are relatively few 'pure' examples of styles otherwise found in great abundance throughout the country. There may be ten buildings of real distinction in Queen Anne style in the entire state, of which perhaps four are noteworthy. Even American Craftsman — a style seemingly well-suited to express the simple but elegant frugality of the early 20th century Southwest — is seldom seen in its full, though understated wardrobe.

The majority of New Mexico's historic buildings, instead, are indigenous in character. Where they are not, some flavor of the native almost always peeks through, whether it be in the adobe core walls or the righteously Italiannate Huning Castle, or the fanciful, if often crude, application of Neo-Greek or Victorian eclectic embellishments to just-plain rural houses of the north country.

Though sometimes trying very hard to look like something more sophisticated, many of New Mexico's older structures are built of adobe. Simple, universal, timeless mud. Adobe construction, in particular, is the focus of the second part of this book, for earth buildings are special preservation challenges: they have an extraordinary propensity for return to their source. That, in an inconvenient sort of way, is part of their beauty.

New Mexico's early buildings are generally very simple, technically and decoratively at least. Prior to the arrival of the railroad and the industrial age, regional architecture had been predicated upon an economy of scarcity. Local resources were used in labor-intensive construction methods. Building massing, land use and town planning all manifested, in one way or another, folk solutions to making a little go far. This tradition seems to have been gradually eroded through the introduction of successive, more recent architectural and town planning strategies. (To get a clearer sense of this evolution, the more detailed discussions of particular buildings concluding each of the following Period chapters contain some commentary on the subject of energy.)

Happily, there is growing interest everywhere in preserving the unique cultural resources embodied in architecture. Some romantic savor of the antique exists in most of us; handcraftsmanship seems especially appealing in an accelerating machine age; a charming, familiar habitat may be a viable line of defense against a growing alienation of man from his natural and cultural environment. And some knowledge of history may also lend inspiration to new, appropriate and conserving philosophies of design, rooted in an understanding of what makes sense for the place. The history of *this* place has a lot to teach.

Zuni Pueblo, as photographed in the late 19th century by Ben Wittick. The town has changed substantially in the last hundred years.
Historically, the Pueblo tradition of vernacular folk-building — like others throughout the pre-industrial world — optimizes characteristics of site and climate for intrinsic building comfort. Built into a south-exposed hillside, the terraces of Zuni open to the south and east, with their backs turned to the cold winter northern winds, and dusty western gusts of spring. (Ben Wittick, Museum of New Mexico Photo Archives)

CHAPTER 1

PUEBLO INDIAN ARCHITECTURE

Among the various cultural threads woven into the fabric of Southwestern architectural history, that of the Indian Pueblos is the oldest, and quite possibly the most celebrated. Pueblo Indian architecture's distinction arises from its large scale and perseverence over a very long period of time, its rational approach to energy and conservation, and from its design integrity and just-plain beauty in folk-vernacular expression.

Though the visual state of most of the pueblos has changed substantially in the last few decades, the framework of a thousand-year building heritage is still apparent: very much so in conservative centers such as Taos, which remains much the same town it was when the Spanish first saw it in the 16th century. Indeed, *pueblo* is the Spanish word for town. It was its architectural and urban sophistication for which the culture became identified, and hundreds of years later, the culture and its impressive architectural tradition are still alive.

Other forms of American Indian architecture are also evident in the Southwest, though none of them is as established — or substantial — as that of the pueblos. Nor have they made as significant an impact on the evolving face of regional style. Some mention of the Plains Indian tepee and the Navajo hogan is made in Chapter 6, "Log Construction."

The development and long history of Pueblo Indian architecture is complex and often elusive. Much remains to be known. Though treated briefly here, the bibliography lists a number of sources which provide a great deal more detail. Probably the most comprehensive historic documentation of the pueblos — 100 years later — is still found in Victor and Cosmos Mindeleffs' *A Study of Pueblo Architecture: Tusayan and Cibola*, published in the Eighth Annual Report of the Bureau of American Ethnology in 1891.

Most of what is known of the prehistoric ancestors of contemporary Pueblo people — and their architectural traditions — is via the vast archaeological resources of the Southwest. The succession of major Puebloan cultural events and building approaches is usually divided into five phases, of which the late and esteemed historian, Bainbridge Bunting, gives a very concise accounting in the introduction to *Early Architecture in New Mexico*:

> *During the Pueblo I and II periods (700 to 900; and 900 to 1050), villages of pithouses evolved into small communities with rows of contiguous, flat-roofed houses built above ground of poles and mud, and then into small towns in which the rectilinear house units were built of stone masonry and sometimes were multistoried. The kiva, an underground ceremonial chamber, became an integral part of each settlement. Advances in the arts and crafts, particularly in pottery making, led to regional specializations. Pueblo III (1050 to 1300) is the Classic period, the apogee of Anasazi culture, when*

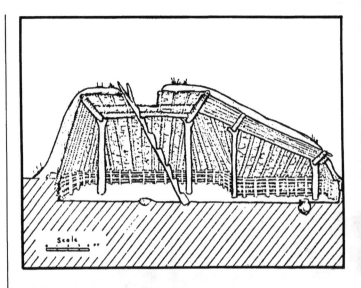

Ninth century pithouse. Simple and energy-efficient structures such as this were built all across the Southwest by Basketmaker ancestors of the Pueblo people. (Martin and Plog, The Archaeology of Arizona.)

Ground plan of Pueblo Bonito at Chaco Canyon. This great prehistoric town, contained within a single massive structure is one of the quintessential examples of Anasazi solar-oriented urban design.

Like a deliberate inversion of the pyramids of central Mexico, a giant crater-like form is created, with up to five levels of houses terracing down toward a central plaza with subterranean religious structures — or kivas. (after Kidder, An Introduction to the Study of Southwestern Archaeology)

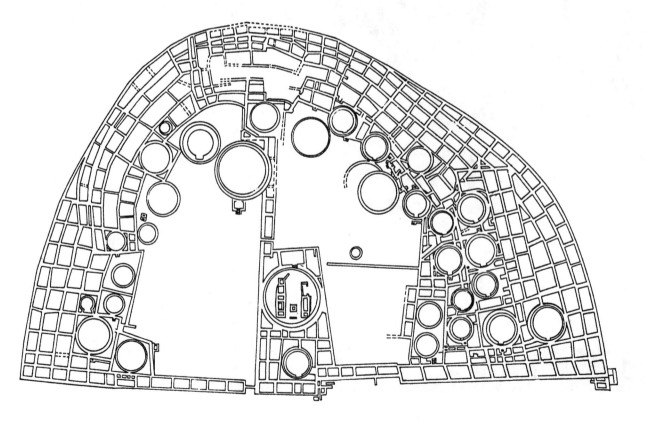

large numbers of people occupied towns of considerable size and social complexity flourished. Peaks were reached in architectural and engineering achievements, in agricultural accomplishments (including water control systems for irrigating arid lands), in the manufacture of goods, pottery vessels, tools, and ornaments, and in the trade of items both within and outside the Anasazi realm.

As a result of numerous factors including pressure from nomadic peoples, depletion of resources, and perhaps social unrest, the heavily populated northern centers of the Anasazi were abandoned around 1300 and over a period of several generations the inhabitants migrated southward to new sites along the Rio Grande and its tributaries or to locations in west central New Mexico and east central Arizona. The Pueblo IV (1350 to about 1700) period not only witnessed a population shift but was marked by cultural regression. Practically all Anasazi activities declined from their previous levels of accomplishment. It was during this time, however, that most pueblos that have survived to the present were established.

Some of these Pueblo IV communities appear to have been moving toward a cultural renaissance when Francisco Vasquez de Coronado led the first Spanish expedition into the Southwest in 1540. Although Christianization of the Indians began even before permanent Spanish colonization in 1598, contact with the Europeans was not close enough to cause marked cultural changes until about 1700, after the return of the Spaniards to the area following the Pueblo Revolt of 1680-93. During the Revolt, Pueblo culture suffered serious dislocations, including a marked population decline due to war, disease, and migrations to join other Indian groups.

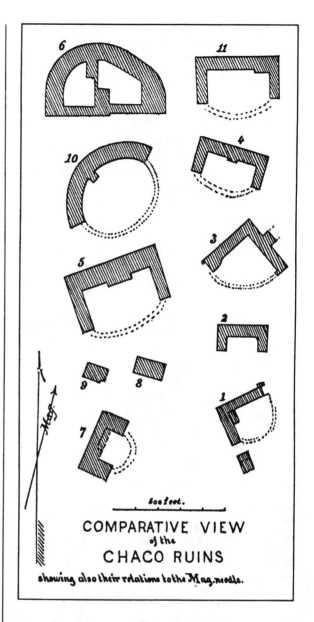

More often than not — though not universally — Anasazi town plans reflect an orientation toward the sun. As single unitized structures, a coherent shape always emerges. By attaching large numbers of "houses" with shared walls, the amount of surface area is minimized, stabilizing interior temperatures. (William Henry Jackson, Tenth Annual Report, U.S. Geological and Geographic Survey, 1878)

As Bunting states, most of today's surviving Indian Pueblos — 19 in New Mexico and 10 in Arizona — were established around 1700, though ancestors had inhabited other settlements in the vicinity for hundreds of years. (The Hopi towns of northern Arizona, unlike those of New Mexco, seldom identify themselves by the term 'Pueblo,' though their architecture and urban morphology clearly illuminate a common cultural heritage.) Some of today's towns are much older — Acoma and Oraibi being inhabited for at least 1000 years — while some, such as Zuni, saw immense growth with a new influx of population after the Reconquest, and a considerable amount of change has occurred since then. Three of the Hopi towns — Hotevilla, Bacavi and Moenkopi — were built in the early 20th century; however, almost every aspect of their planning and architecture reveals the pattern of an ancient tradition

Though 16th and 17th century Spanish mission churches (in all but the Hopi towns, where they were never rebuilt after the Pueblo Revolt) made a monumental imprint on the overall town plan, little Spanish influence is seen in the houses themselves. These were built and maintained much as they had always been, with clustered, terraced massing, centering on the vital 'void,' the plaza: public space of the town, and setting for the all-important religious ceremonials. This common pattern was maintained into the late 19th century, when raiding nomadic tribes were militarily subdued by the new Colonials, the Americans, and the railroad brought a tide of modern goods — and cultural influence.

Traditional construction technique is fundamentally similar throughout the entire Pueblo region, though the nature of local resources creates some variety in the material of wall and roof construction. Also, during the prehistoric era at least, a considerable diversity is apparent in the style and degree of detailing in stonework, and this suggests the nature of cultural migrations and interactions which took place.

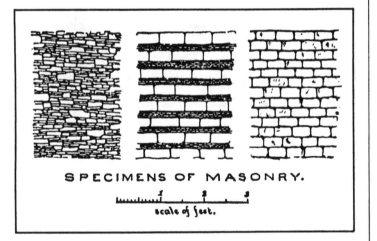

SPECIMENS OF MASONRY.

scale of feet.

Prior to Spanish colonization, walls in villages of the higher, rockier west had been built of stone with small amounts of mud mortar, while walls of settlements along the Rio Grande and its tributaries to the east, were generally of massive, hand-packed earth. The Spaniards seem to have introduced the use of simple stone rubble footings, outdoor baking ovens and interior fireplaces, as well as the technology of forming the same humble earth into bricks — *adobes* — which

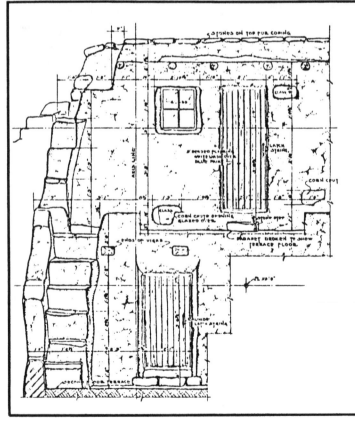

Zuni Pueblo, late 19th century. Many of the hallmark features of historic Pueblo Indian architecture are evident in this photograph, including: terraced construction with flat earth roofs, ladders to connect the various levels, chimney pots — stacks of local pottery with the bottoms removed, and the Spanish-introduced outdoor baking oven (with a ladder pole leaning on top at the bottom of the photo). (Museum of New Mexico Archives)

Three ladders from Hopi, as documented by the Mindeleffs. Similar types of ladders have been excavated at prehistoric sites, establishing their traditional use for several hundred years. (Victor and Cosmos Mindeleff, BAE Eighth Annual Report)

Elevation and section of a house at Acoma, showing characteristic Puebloan construction and the parapet stair especial to the Western pueblos.

Many features derive from prehistoric tradition, though doors and windows here demonstrate Spanish American influence. (Historic American Buildings Survey, 1934)

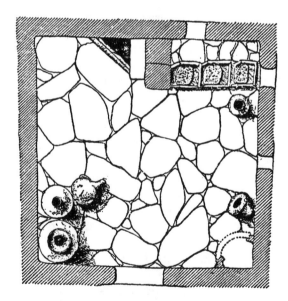

Interior floor plan of an 1880s room at Hopi. Identifiable features include corn-grinding bins (upper right), a corner fireplace (probably, lower right), and pottery jars for storage (lower left). (Victor and Cosmos Mindeleff, BAE Eighth Annual Report)

were dried in the sun and laid in mud mortar.

Roofs were made of peeled logs — or vigas — with smaller poles and brush or reeds laid over them, finished with a dense layer of packed earth. A gradual slope routed water from the flat roofs to drain spouts, or *canales*. Doors and windows were minimal and covered with, if anything, textiles or hides, and later, translucent selenite sheets and hand-adzed, pintled wooden doors. (There is some evidence that selenite, a mica-like mineral, had been used by the prehistoric Anasazi builders of the Pueblo III period. But it had fallen into disuse, and it seems that the Spaniards — with their metal tools to cleave it — reintroduced its use for windows.)

Elements from the American building scene crept in with the 1880s, until today it is rare to find indigenous Pueblo architectural details preserved. The particular elements of this architecture, and succeeding periods, are presented in somewhat more detail in Part II,

This 19th century Zuni interior illustrates the salient features of traditional Puebloan interiors, from left to right: plastered bancos, hooks set in the wall, log and brush ceiling, corn-grinding bins, blanket bar, small interior door, ladder to the roof hatch, hooded fireplace (introduced by the Spanish), and wall niche for storage and display of objects (Victor and Cosmos Mindeleff, BAE Eighth Annual Report)

which addresses historic preservation and conservation.

It may be interesting to note that characteristic construction of the pre-Columbian pueblos — adobe walls and exposed timber roofs — was changed very little by the Spaniards and is carried essentially intact up to the late 19th century. It still forms the basis for more romantic, regionalized construction.

During the past century, and particularly after World War II, density of construction and habitation in the pueblos decreased as many of the towns were suburbanized, and buildings in the older urban cores were abandoned and materials recycled, or they fell into

  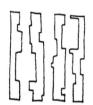

A plaza forms the 'void' core of the traditional Pueblo town plan. With situation and orientation based upon cosmological reference points, the plaza served as the setting for the enactment of religious dances; the space doubled as the 'living room' of the town.

Three main patterns are noticeable in Pueblo plans: First: a casual clustering of house groups in one limited area. There may be one or more plazas, all very irregular; house blocks follow a general pattern of alignment.

Second: more or less regular building around a central plaza or plazas.

Third: rows of parallel house blocks, with space between forming streets which serve the same purpose as the plazas.

 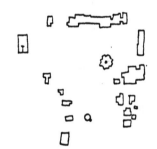

San Ildefonso   1950   San Ildefonso   1975

In some of the Indian pueblos — though the plaza retains its cosmologically-fixed position — the architectural definition of the space is dissolving. With fewer people living on or near the plaza, its function as a vital outdoor communal living room is diminishing also.

At San Ildefonso, a once clearly defined plaza has suffered such disintegration that today, only a few houses on the periphery suggest the historic outlines.

The village of Mishongnovi at Hopi, in northern Arizona in drawings adapted from Mindeleff, shows how the town grew by the addition of subsidiary house rows and plazas. Latest additions suggest the constraints of its rocky citadel site.

Most pueblos have a language of growth by which ensemble is established between old and new, and unity is preserved despite growth.

Taos Pueblo carries the tradition of pueblo architecture into the present more than any of the other towns. Despite substantial changes in door and window treatment, the massing is characteristic of 14th and 15th century types.

The plan of Taos centers two massive terraced house blocks around a large central plaza, through which flows a stream from the sacred Blue Lake, high in the mountains above this important pre-Columbian trading center. (Stanley Stubbs, Birds Eye View of the Pueblos)

LEGEND

☐ 1 STORY
☐ 2 "
☐ 3 "
☐ 4 "
☐ 5 "

···· WALL, OUTLINE ONLY
K KIVA
✝ CHURCH

0   50'   250'

ruin. Stone and adobe walls were frequently replaced with cement block and wood frame; selenite windows were replaced with wood and later, aluminum sash. In most places, change was evident both within the old core and in the suburban accretions.

In certain towns, traditional construction techniques still survive, and in most, the overall character remains distinctively Pueblo. The people value their heritage. The form and scale of the community has not been totally lost, despite a change in massing and architectural details — not to mention changes in social context, including the automobile and a wage-economy. Fortunately for some of the Indian Pueblos, an increasing sensitivity to the importance of their built heritage has fostered encouraging, and sometimes innovative, efforts toward adaptive reuse and historic preservation. The nature — and value — of this contemporary renaissance in Pueblo design was celebrated in the 1980s by an opus touring exhibition, *The Center Space: Pueblo Indian Architecture* — an expression of the growing interest in history and preservation throughout the United States. The impact, motives and mechanics of this movement are explored in Parts II and III.

ARCHITECTURE AND ENERGY IN THE PUEBLOS

Typical of building traditions in other pre-industrial societies, architecture of the Southwest's historic Indian Pueblos frequently exhibits climatically well-attuned siting and construction considerations. Though later and surviving towns generally do not measure as well as prehistoric antecedants — notably the great Anasazi urban megastructures — they still preserve some of their simple passive solar characteristics. An early town, dating roughly from A.D. 1000 (and surviving today), Acoma Pueblo is the subject of a brief energy analysis which concludes this chapter.

A more detailed, if not exhaustive, view of a particular site — in terms of energy, cultural perspective and style — concludes each of the following chapters in Part I. Attitudes about resources and technology — and their uses — can lend deeper insights into the overt manifestations of historic or regional style. Particularly in earlier, less self-

conscious styles, generated within an economy of scarcity — the 'vernacular' — there is almost always the reflection of an enduring folk-wisdom.

The basic world view of Pueblo people seems to have a lot to do with the nature of their town planning and architecture. Traditional Puebloans see themselves and their society as part of a larger, comprehensive, sacred ecosystem. Wanton resource exploitation is unthinkable. As such, all things were historically cherished and conserved. Rainwater was collected or carefully diverted to irrigation. Every cloud and every season were cause to acknowledge and implore cooperation with the elements. Within the challenging natural ecology of the region, cooperation, intensification and 'miniaturization' (to borrow a word from contemporary Southwestern urban theorist, Paolo Soleri, who seems to be rediscovering the wisdom of regional antiquity) is manifested in Pueblo Indian architecture. This sensibility, and its built artifacts, fostered and sustained a people of deeper cultural development, stability and productivity than anyone else in the area for hundreds of years. Now, for the evidence.

The Pueblo of Acoma today best preserves what we might call the 'Anasazi Section'; that is, a row of attached houses, terraced floor-by-floor in a southerly orien-

Cliff Palace at Mesa Verde. The Anasazi also built in shallow natural caves, which provided security and shelter from the elements.

Those natural caves which faced toward the south were preferred, though other orientations were also used. At Cliff Palace, the low winter sun floods the high mass stone walls with warmth, while in the summer, the cliff overhang provides shade from the higher angle of the sun. (David Mussina)

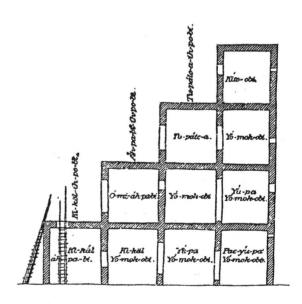

Mindeleffs' diagram showing the ideal section of Hopi houses. Each of the terraces and adjacent rooms is identified by Hopi names. More often than not, the terraces face to the south, or sometimes east. (Victor and Cosmos Mindeleff, BAE Eighth Annual Report)

tation. Other villages, such as Taos or historic Zuni exhibit a similar section, but it is less pure in apparent form. (According to historical record, at the time of Spanish conquest, Acoma also had rows of houses in an area later occupied by the large mission church. These ran north and south, and probably terraced toward the east; maybe the west; maybe both directions. This pattern is more like that of Hopi Oraibi, also occupied since about A.D. 1000; clear evidence that Pueblo Indian town plans were not always optimally solar-oriented. So much for glamorized history!)

Ralph Knowles and architecture students at the University of Southern California prepared a study — *Energy and Form*, MIT Press, 1974 — in which an evaluation was made of solar considerations in the existing urban configuration of Acoma Pueblo. It clearly demonstrated the intention of climatically-tempered design. The study found that several factors contributed to Acoma's success in passive solar utilization:

Acoma's three major house rows feature attached, party-wall buildings; most east and west walls are shared with other houses. The volume is enclosed by a significantly smaller surface than, say, detached houses. With less surface area exposed to heat gain and loss, interior temperatures tend to be stabilized. Also, less material and labor would be required in construction.

The axis of the rows is a few degrees east of due south, with the rows critically spaced to maximize winter solar gain, and minimize shading on the long south elevations.

The houses, typically three stories high, terrace toward the south and have a high, massive north wall, creating the most surface where it would collect winter sun, and the least where it would not be advantageous The north wall would be both a heat-loss liability in the winter, and a heat-gain liability in the summer, when the sun strikes it early and late in the day. Its area is kept to a minimum.

Almost all doors and windows open on-

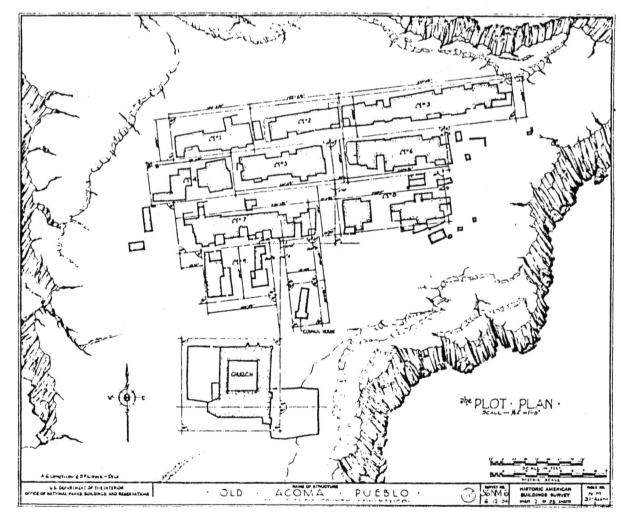

Acoma Pueblo. At historic Acoma, houses terrace toward the south in long, continuous rows: the best exposure for catching the low winter sun. The design is impressive — within the constraints of native building technology — in its use of solar energy. Within a clear pattern, variety is seen in the architectural particulars of each house.

Reservoirs collect water from the rocky citadel site, where it is put to domestic use, and sacred springs nested along the base of the mesa provide fresh water for drinking.

Site plan of Acoma Pueblo. (Historic American Buildings Survey, *1934)*

Plan and elevations of one of the Acoma house blocks. (Historic American Buildings Survey, *1934)*

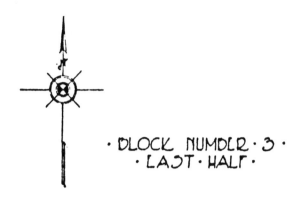

· BLOCK · NUMBER · 3 ·
· LAST · HALF ·

· EAST · ELEVATION ·

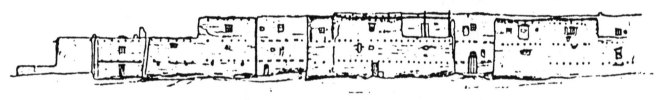

· NORTH · ELEVATION ·

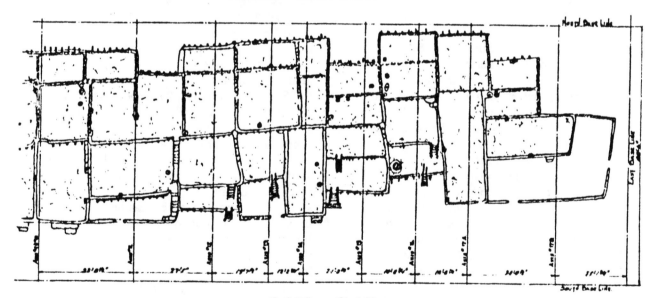

· ROOF · PLAN ·

· SOUTH · ELEVATION ·

21

to the south terraces, with very few openings on the north.

Walls between the units usually extend above the roof for 2 to 4 feet, reducing the impact of wind; and south-roof overhangs (of optimal summer shading depth) create wind-protected solar "collecting pans."

As the south wall is at a better angle of incidence (more perpendicular) to the low winter sun, it might be expected that it would be of a high-mass, heat collecting and transmitting material; with adobe and stone construction, it is.

The high summer sun bears more directly on the flat earth roofs, so it would be logical to have a heat-absorptive construction which provides some insulation, and re-radiates summer heat to the night sky. Taking the wood and brush fill below the finish earth into account, it seems to provide these qualities.

The study reveals what the Indians must have understood for the past thousand years: the pueblo is an energy efficient system that tends to equalize internal energy profiles over the extremes of season and day. By its shape and materials, it provides an internal consistency, a steady state.

This analysis of Acoma — theoretical and not based on actual thermal monitering — concludes that the town structure is about 50% more efficient in its use of potential solar energy in the winter than in the summer: pretty impressive, given the simple means of construction and a very limited range of materials.

Acoma is at the optimal end of the scale in terms of energy-efficient urban design among the historic Indian pueblos. Most are somewhere in the middle. Few, if any, are at the lower end, i.e., occupying northerly slopes with north-facing terraces or individual, detached houses. Recent generations of government-initiated housing programs in the pueblos have not been so wise in their siting and massing strategy. But Pueblo people are now rediscovering the proven sense of their heritage and are demanding — and, one hopes, getting — more responsive and intelligent approaches to environmental design

From the ancient foundation of Pueblo Indian architecture, the history of building in the Southwest unfolds. The enduring Pueblo tradition overlaps it all. Every people, every style. Each new cultural tide, and each new generation has brought with it ideas about how buildings should look, and how they should work. By and large, though architecture has assumed an increasing sense of stylistic posture, not much has been done to improve on the fundamental tradition of an innate conservation design-awareness, as witnessed in the prehistoric and even historic Indian pueblos. As Part I of this book concludes, with Chapter 7, a new movement in modern regionalism — manifested in contemporary solar-adobe design — seems to be bringing historic regional precedent and modern technology together. But several chapters and a few hundred years in the historic chronology lie in between.

El Plaza del Cerro, Chimayo, New Mexico. Built before 1760, this is the best surviving example of the Spanish Colonial plaza-type town. Though only this western side of the compound retains the flat roofs of early construction, the overall urban form is still apparent.

The other sides of the plaza conform, more or less, to the original lines, but have been modified with pitched roofs. Throughout the town, a splendid variety of Territorial-primitive Greek Revival details may be seen in door and window treatments. (Melinda Bell, Museum of New Mexico Photo Archives)

CHAPTER 2

SPANISH COLONIAL & MEXICAN ARCHITECTURE

A substantial part of New Mexico's unique architectural character was forged during the Spanish Colonial and subsequent Mexican periods (1598 - 1846). Though virtually no unaltered buildings exist from these years, documentation suggests that the same general types were built from the first Spanish settlement of San Gabriel, near present San Juan Pueblo in 1598, up through the Mexican period of 1823 - 1846.

The conservative and marginal atmosphere of the northern colonial frontier was perpetuated, if not rendered even more extreme, after Mexico's independence from Spain. As there appears to be essentially no change in architecture during the two short decades of the Mexican period, it is included, for the purposes of this review, together with Spanish Colonial. Together, they form a continuum of 250 years of what we presume is essentially one sustained tradition. The best surviving examples of Spanish Colonial architecture are found in mission churches in the Indian pueblos and rural Spanish towns, and in haciendas and smaller houses of the outlying farm lands of the north. The Rio Abajo to the south also retains a few good examples along the major historic road to Mexico.

The Palace of the Governors, in Santa Fe, dates from the establishment of the Colonial capital in that *villa* in 1610. The Palace is the oldest public building in the United States (only, however, if one does not consider as public the great communal house blocks of some of the Indian pueblos). Though dating from the very early Spanish Colonial period, it has received so many modifications, and several partial reconstructions in its almost 400 years, that little of its true 17th century

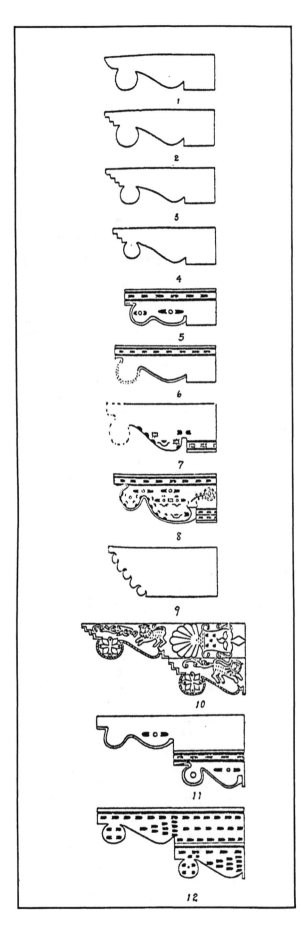

fabric remains.

Early Spanish construction technology was much like that of the indigenous Pueblo Indians: thick earth, or occasionally stone or sod block walls, with flat earth roofs, laid over ceiling beams of peeled logs, or *vigas*. While the Indians had used puddled adobe for construction of walls, the Spaniards seem to to have introduced the technology of forming adobe — a mixture of clay, sand, water and often straw or other plant fiber — into bricks, which were then sun-dried. (Somehow without much confusion, in New Mexico lingo, adobe can refer to either the mud mixture, the brick itself, or even whole buildings of the material.)

During the Spanish Colonial era, other refinements were also introduced, such as squared, hand-adzed roof beams, and some simple cabinetwork. Occasionally with hand-carving and decorative painting, these elements were usually reserved for churches and important rooms in prominent dwellings. A limited amount of free-standing furniture also appeared, together with developments in fireplace and chimney design.

Whereas the Puebloans had customarily built walls directly on the earth, the Spaniards preferred the use of simple stone rubble footings. Though limited in their ability to structurally support the massive weight, they at least reduced the destructive impact of water on the base of the wall. *Jacal*, or wattle-and-daub — a combination of wood, brush and mud — was also used, primarily for ancillary or farm buildings. Horizontal and vertical log construction was employed in certain highland locales. But the simple, handmade mud brick seems to have been the decided preference.

Window and door openings were very, very limited, both for security and temperature control. They were usually covered only by pintled wooden shutters, in which the top and bottom on one side are extended as rough pins to fit into sockets in the sill and lintel. Some hand-forged hinges, latches and other hardware are also found from this period, but rather seldom. Selenite (mica slabs), as seen at Acoma and Taos Pueblos today, was prob-

Spanish Colonial corbels in a variety of elaborations. As true corbels, these would be engaged in the wall though the design might be repeated in mirror image for column capitals. (Sylvanus Morley, "Santa Fe Architecture," 1914-15)

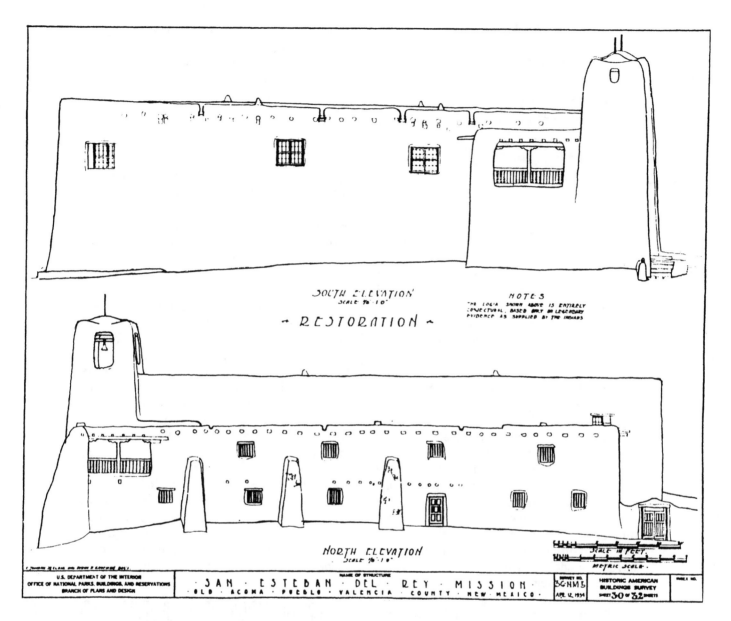

SOUTH ELEVATION
Scale ⅛"= 1'0"

~ RESTORATION ~

NOTES
THE LOGIA SHOWN ABOVE IS ENTIRELY
CONJECTURAL, BASED ONLY ON LEGENDARY
EVIDENCE AS SUPPLIED BY THE INDIANS

NORTH ELEVATION
Scale ⅛"= 1'0"

SCALE IN FEET

METRIC SCALE

U.S. DEPARTMENT OF THE INTERIOR
OFFICE OF NATIONAL PARKS, BUILDINGS, AND RESERVATIONS
BRANCH OF PLANS AND DESIGN

NAME OF STRUCTURE
· S A N · E S T E B A N · D E L · R E Y · M I S S I O N ·
· O L D · A C O M A · P U E B L O · V A L E N C I A · C O U N T Y · N E W · M E X I C O ·

SURVEY NO.
36-NM-5
APR. 12, 1934

HISTORIC AMERICAN
BUILDINGS SURVEY
SHEET 30 OF 32 SHEETS

INDEX NO.

ably the only glazing available until the 19th century, though no early Spanish houses are known to have surviving examples. A more complete description of the evolution of these and other elements of building technology can be found in Part II of this book.

Floor plans in the Spanish Colonial period were almost always a contiguous sequence of rooms in single file, one room deep. The width of rooms is fairly standard at about 15 feet — established by the reasonable span of a log of moderate size. The absence of wider plans, two or more rooms deep — which would have been technically feasible, and can be seen in the Indian pueblos of the same period — is noteworthy. Presumedly, this long, thin pattern grows out of the directive of cultural tradition, rooted in the desire

to stretch plan length to the maximum, in order to enclose space. This attenuated pattern of floor plan is evident in both individual houses and whole town plans of the 16th to mid-19th centuries.

As originally established, Spanish towns were enclosed, fortified compounds: the attached houses themselves defined a large interior square and opened onto it. The continuous outside wall was completely solid, with no doors or windows, and the entire town was entered through large gates into the central courtyard. Under the duress of Indian attack, livestock could be corralled in the enclosure and the whole establishment defended from the flat roofs. The *torreon* also appears to have been a characteristic feature: a usually round, two-story tower explicitly

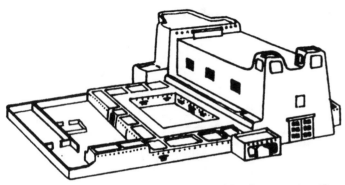

Church and convento of San Buenaventura, Gran Quivira National Monument, as it may have appeared about 1665. (National Park Service, U.S. Department of the Interior)

for the purpose of final defense. The town now known as Dixon had at least two of them at corners of the enclosing house rows.

Though most of Chimayo's buildings have had Territorial and later door and window revisions, and pitched roofs added, it is certainly the preeminent surviving example of Spanish Colonial town planning. Other fragmentary examples can be seen at Trampas, Dixon, El Rito and San Miguel and Villanueva in the region of Pecos.

Today we refer to the void, enclosed space as a *plaza*; but originally, plaza referred to the entire town, as a consistent urban type. Its configuration was decreed by the Spanish Crown down to orientation and dimensions. However, few actual sites conformed to official specifications, and seem to have responded, instead, to the builders sensibilities with regard to the nature of the site and the needs of the population.

For at least 150 years, virtually every one of the colonial Spaniards lived in plaza-type towns, or sometimes in the Indian pueblos themselves, particularly during periods of heavy harassments by raiding nomadic Indians. Taos Pueblo had harbored Spanish-speaking settlers within its defensive walls during the 1770s, until it was safe to return to their own towns.

The *hacienda* is another, probably later, type which represents a kind of miniature plaza or *plazuela*. A particularly landed family might have a large house nearer their fields, and its plan followed closely on the town type — a string of contiguous rooms defining

Georgian window on the Ranchos de Taos Church. Though almost all Spanish Colonial and Mexican period buildings have had windows changed, this is among the most distinctive of adaptations.

a central enclosed space — on a smaller scale. Just the same, the number of rooms necessary to create such a plan is considerable and very few families had such resources.

Four major haciendas are known to have existed in the Taos Ranchitos area, and each must have had the capacity for its own defense. The least altered example of the Colonial hacienda is probably the Pascual Martinez house in Ranchitos de Taos (In the 1980s, this building is undergoing a major restoration/reconstruction to its early 19th century character, albeit occasionally hypothetical. Despite criticism on this count, it should prove illuminating.) Another largely conjectural, but very captivating reconstruction is Rancho de las Golondrinas near La Cienega, southwest of Santa Fe.

More common in this later period would have been a much smaller house, without a floor area large enough to fully enclose an interior plazuela. The region where this type is most widely seen today is the northern highland valleys of Penasco, Trampas and Truchas. Smaller buildings, on the higher lands above family fields, these had little specialized room use, with cooking, eating, living and sleeping sharing functions within the same spaces. The *sala*, or formal living room (simple though it was,) seems to have been the first room endowed with a special use designation. As a family grew or its fortunes improved, additional rooms would be added to the typical single file, slowly grow-

ing in a manner which evolved toward the eventual prospect of an enclosed plazuela.

The Manuel Atencio house in Trampas, built from about 1820 until its final addition in 1912, is a good example of this later type of rural house, though it was still close enough to the fortified town to have been afforded some defensive security. Characteristic of other buildings in Trampas, the Atencio house features upswept parapet corners and the absence of otherwise typical projecting vigas, lending this structure and others in the Trampas area a particular purity of sculptural form.

The Atencio house clearly exhibits well the concerns and approaches to conservation in the Spanish Colonial and Mexican periods. (Though some of its parts date from later periods, they seem still to have followed on traditional regional types.) Typical of early 19th century buildings in the northern highlands, the Atencio house has a number of characteristics which demonstrate sensible site and climatic response:

The Ranchos de Taos church. A classic example of the sculptural potential of earth architecture, at its primal, expressive best.

• The house is sited on a south-exposed slope, above an irrigation ditch, preserving the arable land below for agriculture.
• The building is cut into the slope of the hill, with the north wall partially buried into the earth, for effective insulation and reduced exposure to chilling winter winds from the north.
• The walls and roof are of high-mass adobe, conveniently available on the site and well suited to the extremes of mountain valley climate. (For data on adobe's thermal performance, see 'Walls' and 'Roofs,' Part II.)
• The axis of the house is stretched roughly east-west, to maximize solar exposure of the long south wall; most doors and windows are located for this southern exposure.
• When a wing was added in the mid-1880s, it was to the southwest: the best location to deflect prevailing winds coming up the valley
• Although fireplaces in the Atencio house

27

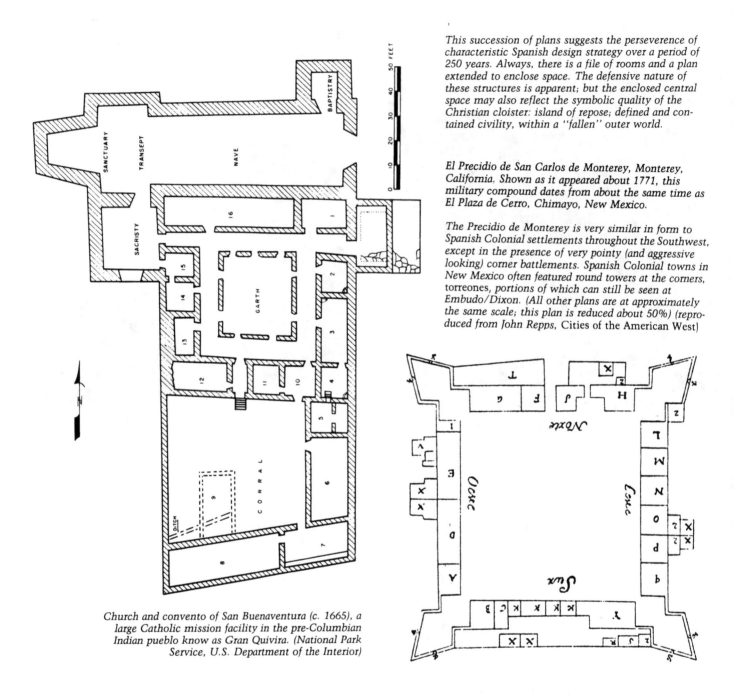

This succession of plans suggests the perseverence of characteristic Spanish design strategy over a period of 250 years. Always, there is a file of rooms and a plan extended to enclose space. The defensive nature of these structures is apparent; but the enclosed central space may also reflect the symbolic quality of the Christian cloister: island of repose; defined and contained civility, within a "fallen" outer world.

El Precidio de San Carlos de Monterey, Monterey, California. Shown as it appeared about 1771, this military compound dates from about the same time as *El Plaza de Cerro, Chimayo, New Mexico.*

The Precidio de Monterey is very similar in form to Spanish Colonial settlements throughout the Southwest, except in the presence of very pointy (and aggressive looking) corner battlements. Spanish Colonial towns in New Mexico often featured round towers at the corners, torreones, portions of which can still be seen at Embudo/Dixon. (All other plans are at approximately the same scale; this plan is reduced about 50%) (reproduced from John Repps, Cities of the American West)

Church and convento of San Buenaventura (c. 1665), a large Catholic mission facility in the pre-Columbian Indian pueblo know as Gran Quivira. (National Park Service, U.S. Department of the Interior)

have been removed and replaced by wood stoves, other buildings of the period suggest that they would have been at interior corners, on walls shared by two rooms: not on exterior corners, as so often seen in the Pueblo Revival (a derivative architecture which values stylistic potential over thermal efficiency).

While comfort levels of these early Spanish houses and towns were certainly substantially lower than contemporary standards, concern for optimizing the characteristics of site, materials and climate is apparent. Cutting

and hauling firewood was tedious, stands of timber receding ever further, and sharpening the costly hand-forged metal tools was doubtless a chore. Though the east-west axis, south-oriented building is frequent but not universal in the Colonial and Mexican period, it is perhaps worth noting its similarity to some contemporary solar-adobe designs.

The frontier colonist *had* to build in a conserving manner. This basic indigenous type of house was a reasonably good solution: a not-unsimilar model was built in the 1970s at the Ghost Ranch Sundwellings Demon-

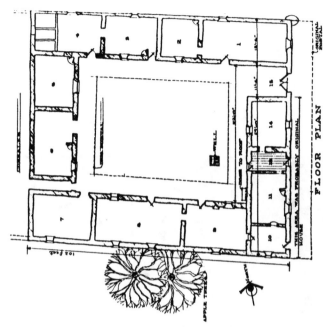

The Pascual Martinez house, Ranchitos de Taos, a large private hacienda dating from the early 19th century. (Fort Burgwin Research Center, Southern Methodist University, published in Bainbridge Bunting's Taos Adobes)

The Manuel Atencio house (ca. 1820, with later additions): a rural, single-file farmhouse on the western watershed of the Sangre de Cristos.

This classic example of late Spanish Colonial homestead grew over time, with each addition conforming to an apparent, and climate-conscious, vocabulary of form. (Fort Burgwin Research Center, Southern Methodist University)

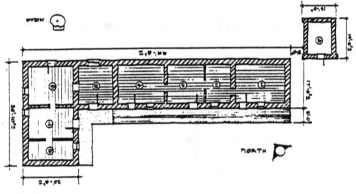

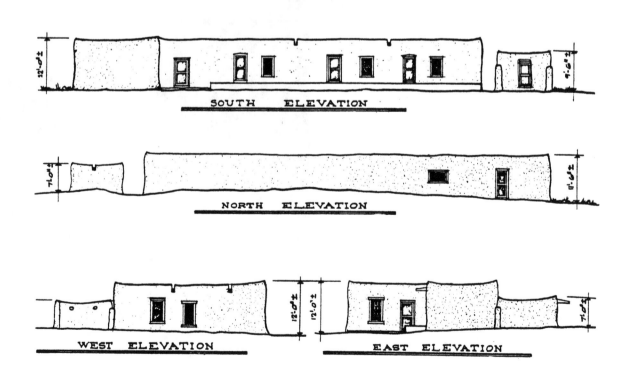

SOUTH ELEVATION

NORTH ELEVATION

WEST ELEVATION

EAST ELEVATION

stration Center, and it was proven to be 28% efficient in passive solar performance. (See page 105).

But by the mid-19th century, Americans were arriving in greater numbers; with them came not only new materials and technology, but also a new resource ethic. Centuries of Indian and Spanish conservation techniques, bred in austerity, were soon to be visited by a new amenity...and unprecedented patterns of consumption.

The Borrego house, Canyon Road, Santa Fe. Built before 1769, this early house is typical of many Spanish Colonial buildings which received the new style with grace and ease. (D. Orton Smith, Museum of New Mexico Photo Archives)

CHAPTER 3

TERRITORIAL STYLE

The Territorial period begins in 1846, with the annexation of New Mexico into the United States, and the entrance of Brigadier General Stephen Watts Kearny and the U.S. Army into the new Territory. In *Early Architecture in New Mexico*, Bainbridge Bunting divides the period into three major sections. These are Early, from territoriality to the end of the Civil War (1848 - 1865); Middle, the period after the war, when commerce and cultural interaction were flourishing (1865 -1880); and Late, after the arrival of the railroad and its profusion of imported styles, until statehood (1880 - 1912).

Between 1821, with Mexican independence from Spain and the opening of the Santa Fe Trail, and 1880, when the railroad entirely supplanted the Trail, the West saw an ever-increasing tide of American influence. It was the Santa Fe Trail, in function and in idea, which was the vehicle for and foundation of the Territorial style. Glass could be bought from the Midwest; local production of brick and milled lumber was established: these provided for technically improved architecture. But with a new government in 1846, a new style was in order and it was Greek Revival.

The recurring, simplifying inspiration of Neoclassicism had arrived to rescue Europe from the Baroque by the late 1770s, and it was soon introduced into the United States. Pinnacle achievements like Thomas Jefferson's designs for the University of Virginia and Monticello aptly expressed the vision of the New Republic.

From about 1820 until 1850, Greek Revival was all the rage in the East. As it migrated through the Midwest and South, it usually began in a fairly rustic mode, but was swiftly civilized. By the time of the Civil War, Neo-Greek had become fairly passe in the East, but it was still going strong in the provinces. Eventually, formal Greek compositional motifs — colonnade, pediment and cornice — pushed west with the wagon train, and slipped gently over the flat-roofed, earth-walled buildings of local tradition.

The style caught on almost universally on "sophisticated" new construction, and was widely adapted to older, existing single-file Spanish and Mexican period houses, probably for several reasons. First, the advent of doors and windows significantly enhanced the comfort of the native architecture, as far as lighting and ventilation were concerned. Naturally, people wanted them. The Greek rendition evidenced in earliest examples of these new refinements would suggest that, if you wanted doors and windows, this is how it would be done, though they could almost as easily have been Romanesque or something else.

Second, the imagery was somehow appropriate. Neoclassicism is a recurrent motif in

A great antebellum mansion in Little Rock, Arkansas. Built in the last years before the Civil War, this house has a Classical correctness that most earlier, local 'developmental' designs lack. Like buildings on the Western frontier 50 years later, the introduction of the first Greek Revival in the South had often involved the remodelling of earlier (French) colonial buildings.

Exterior view of Monticello. (The Georgian Colonial Period, *1902*)

Imperial architecture, like British Colonial buildings of the late 19th century in India or Egypt (or, for that matter, Albert Spier's designs for monuments to the Third Reich). Allusions to the Greek and Roman Republics and their edifices seem often to reflect a righteous adherence to a belief in manifest destiny, which in its time motivated, or at least rationalized, the steamroller of westward expansionism. Pioneer images of culture and progress were materialized in neo-Greek architecture.

Third, the new style could be extraordinarily beautiful. Judging from its emulation even today, it would have to be considered a very winning formulation.

The Territorial marriage of materials and styles — indigenous and Greek — could achieve stunning effects of contrast and harmony. The Classical idea of building as 'object in the landscape' — mathematical, pure and abstract — might have completely overwhelmed the earthy simplicity of the existing vernacular; instead, frontier austerity demanded that a considerable amount of the native vocabulary be retained. In classic Territorial, the traditional earth itself rises to form shelter in walls and roof, and on this organic envelope hover the crisp white pediment and colonnade. While the ultimate appearance of Territorial is a significant departure from earlier construction, it is important

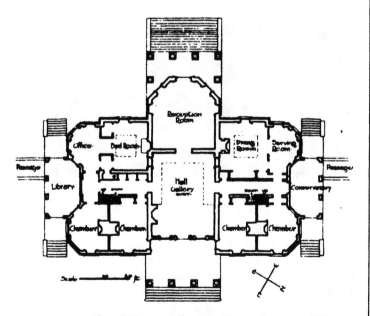

Plan of Thomas Jefferson's Monticello, in rural Virginia (1772). Centralized, symmetrical plans were typical of the Neoclassicism of the Federal style. (the Georgian Colonial Period, 1902)

to note, however, that the basic technical solution to adobe construction did not change significantly for another three decades after its introduction.

Three specific contributions were crucial to the development of Territorial architecture: window glass, milled lumber and brick. Together with a different prevailing mentality and the new defensive security, such as it was, of a military territory, these showed up in buildings as: new, deeper plan types, with central halls; the elaboration of doors and windows as explicit compositional elements; squared, roughly classical columns and other interior and exterior woodwork, usually painted white; pitched roofs; brick coping on the top of the adobe parapet walls, and later, all-brick buildings; and the advent — beyond earlier Indian and Spanish religious structures — of discrete institutional and commercial buildings.

Window glass (brought by wagons across the Santa Fe Trail) is first documented in use on the Customs House, which was on the east side of the Santa Fe Plaza by 1837, during the Mexican period. It is known to have existed in the Palace of the Governors by 1846. Since these were important public buildings, they would likely represent some of the earliest uses of glass in the region. As transportation across the Santa Fe Trail became more routine after the Civil War, the extent of glass and the size of the separate panes became larger.

Another key development in territorial architecture was the establishment of sawmills in several areas, to service army needs. These included Santa Fe (Fort Marcy), Mora and Watrus/La Junta (Fort Union) by 1851. Lumber became commercially available shortly thereafter, but was sparingly used up until the late 19th century. Applications of milled wood in the period include door and window frames and cases, detailed porch woodwork and framing for pitched roofs.

Pitched roofs had been used on pre-Civil War buildings in rural mountain areas where wood was plentiful. Now, sawn lumber permitted their widespread adaptation to the native architecture elsewhere. Especially in lower elevation areas where precipitation is less frequent and stands of good timber are some distance away, flat roofs of earth construction continued to be used. But in northern and higher elevation areas, hipped and

33

Detail of the Clawson House, San Miguel del Vado (photographed during renovation in the early 1980s).

The barebones of the Southwest's Territorial style are evident in this 1855 modernization of an older plazuela type Spanish Colonial house, where only the front facade and major rooms were thus embellished. Colonade and window pediment recall similar features as seen in Monticello, but on a much smaller, and rustic, scale.

Doorway of the Professor J.A. Wood house in Santa Fe. A stately elegance is achieved, despite failure of the individual glazing treatments to match exactly. They seldom do match in period 19th century 'frontier Greek,' but an imposing image is achieved anyway.

gabled roofs gained widespread popularity. They provided significant insulating and waterproofing improvements over earlier construction. Typical pitches, as they vary from area to area, generally reflect levels of precipitation; higher and wetter locales tend to produce steeper roofs, while lower, dryer elevations tend toward lower pitched roofs.

Pitched roofs were framed with milled lumber and surfaced with sawn boards in a lapped pattern, like board and batten or with split shingles. Over the Santa Fe Trail came terne plate metal in sheets, which were assembled on site. Later came corrugated iron, standing seam panels, and pressed decorative plate metals. Later still came asbestos and asphalt shingles and roll roofing.

Wood-framed pitched roofs were often added directly over existing flat earth roofs. This solution provided for both the benefits of high thermal mass in the older earth roof, and some insulation provided by the enclosed attic space (which was seldom used for anything but storage). Of course, the principal objective was to shed water, which quickly compromises any form of earth construction. This it did well, so the pitched roof was adopted almost universally in certain areas,

becoming a characteristic feature of an established sub-regional style. The old plaza at Chimayo is an excellent example of attached buildings in this genre, containing a beautiful array of folk-territorial detail. (A following section on the Mountain Gabled Style contains a more complete description of this particular variation).

Doorways and windows witnessed substantial changes during this period, both in their detail execution and in their contribution to overall architectural intent. While earlier doors and windows had been, in essence, minimal and rather random holes in walls — perhaps with a hand-adzed door, but more likely covered with textiles or hides — they not became prominent elements of a composed facade. Symmetry made new advances as a deliberate, formal compositional device. This was reflected in new developments in floor plans, carrying the focus of a central door into a central hall.

Interior and exterior window and door casings were often quite plain, distinguished more by their contrasting paint than classical 'correctness.' Pedimented top framing boards on windows and doors were usually simple flat tri-angles, cut from milled lumber. Later, mouldings were brought over the Trail for cornice detailing on finer buildings.

Pueblo Indian and Spanish architecture had already produced the colonnaded *portal*, or

Adobe house in the Nambe Valley, northern New Mexico. Even without the customary brick coping, the signature of Territorial is evident in door and window treatment. The soft contour of mud plaster (still maintained) lends a striking contrast to the crisp while detailing.

Officer's house at Fort Marcy, Santa Fe. Pitched metal roofs are typical of military buildings in the Territorial period, but are less frequently associated with the style in the architectural vocabulary of later revivals. (U.S. Army Signal Corps, Museum of New Mexico Photo Archives).

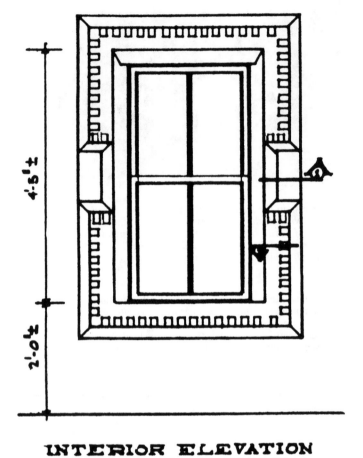

INTERIOR ELEVATION OF WINDOW IN ROOM 1

1" = 1'-0"

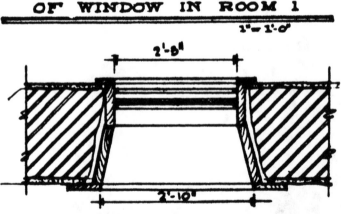

This window detail from the Atencio house in Las Trampas shows the lunatic abandon with which vernacular builders adapted regimented classical forms in totally imprecise — and often amusing ways.

Only two quoins (usually major building corner blocks) are used, and these hover at mid-sash, while the dentiles — always horizontal and always beneath a cornice on "proper" architecture — ramble full-circuit around the frame. (Fort Burgwin Research Center, Southern Methodist University)

porch, executed with round log columns, and usually some form of capital detail. The Territorial style now elaborated this feature with a more imposing intention. Columns were now square cut, often with chamfered corners, and applied moldings, completed the effect of a simple, usually vaguely Doric, capital.

Like door and window casings, these columns and *portales* were generally fairly primitive versions of the classical orders, though many early examples achieved real elegance with an economy of means. Primitivism, in itself, does not necessarily denote early construction however, as simple means were always employed in more remote areas, and variations on the Territorial theme continue to this day (often at the hands of architects and builders who appear as ignorant of good Greek as were their frontier predecessors). Even though the majority of older buildings are quite rudimentary in their Greek Revival allusions, occasionally to the point of visual humor, most of these still compare favorably with some of the overblown and frequently uninformed examples created in other provincial regions only a few years earlier, notably the Deep South.

Brick kilns were established in Las Vegas, Santa Fe and Albuquerque during the early years of the Territorial period, and they provided the material for the third key element in the style: dentiled brick copings capping the parapet wall. Erosion at the top of adobe walls had been a persistent problem in the preceding architecture; occasionally, flat stones were placed on the top of the wall to reduce erosion. But several courses of brick, laid in mortar, proved to be a significant improvement. (A good number of period buildings do not include this charactertistic element, though with pedimented doors and windows, the style still reads 'Territorial.')

A variety of patterns were incorporated in the successive layering of the brick courses. An end-to-end stringer course generally was laid first on the adobe wall, and somewhere in the middle of the built-up section, a course usually appeared with bricks laid alternately in and out — or diagonally set in a sawtooth — which roughly emulates the teeth of a Greek dentiled cornice Interestingly, this Greek dentiled cornice is in no case known to have been painted white, though the other Neoclassical elements virtually always were. By carrying this one element into the natural palette of the walls, earth and brick itself, the Territorial style achieved a subtle balance between the classical "building-as-object" idea, and the landscape-integration of native tradition.

Later, brick was used in the construction of entire walls, and though more permanent, it was considered more costly than adobe. Brick wall construction continued into the eclectic railroad period and beyond. Most buildings, however, continued to be built with adobe walls, if not roofs. To be sure, many buildings went to great effort not to appear to be mud. The Pinckney Tully House in

The Tully house, like some other buildings of the Territorial period, went to great lengths not to appear like the lowly adobe of regional tradition. Here, the entire (actually adobe) building was meticulously painted to look like red brick, including appropriate lintel details at doors and windows.

Nicely executed details of column and brick 'denticulated' (toothed) cornice, on the Pinckney Tully House, Santa Fe (1851).

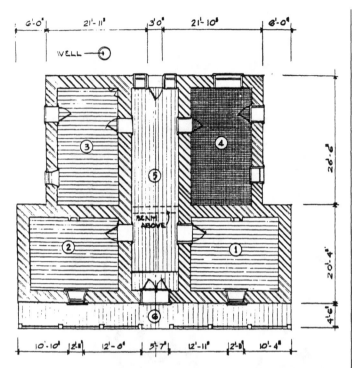

Floor plan of the Leandro Martinez House, Ranchitos de Taos, in northern New Mexico. Like Monticello, the symmetrical plan is organized around a central hall. Though new in the Territorial period, this layout was imposed on many existing buildings, and became characteristic for new buildings. (Fort Burgwin Research Center, Southern Methodist University)

Santa Fe (1851) received a hard plaster entirely painted to look like brand new red brick, including courses with mortar, keystone arches, lintels, and so forth. The house is now restored, and the overall effect is so startling that many people cannot believe it represents an historic treatment. Indeed, many adobe buildings were curiously dressed up during the Territorial period, including the earlier Palace of the Governors, painted to look like large limestone blocks.

A new type of floor plan was introduced in the Territorial period, with central hall, and a generally more complex spatial order than earlier regional models. The 'one-dimensional' string of rooms becomes a two-dimensional grid. Taking a variety of configurations — L, T, U or completely enclosed placita, the traditional plan had been seldom more than one room deep. With the new squarer plan, buildings now had the prospect of extending deeper into the site; this pattern was probably influenced by the shape of city lots, on which some of the earlier military and residential Territorial period houses were constructed. The central hall, even when it

now appeared in single-file buildings, was a natural extension of the new concept of the centralized, composed facade.

Interiors of Territorial buildings, likewise received a considerable elaboration over previous types. They were better lit and better ventilated, and more articulated — and perhaps functional — in zoning. New materials and technology afforded the development of squared ceiling beams, wood floors (to replace earth), and a considerable advance in the degree of finish cabinetwork, including door and window casings and shutters. Fireplaces sometimes moved from traditional corner locations into the center of the wall, more along the lines of Eastern and Midwestern tastes, and generally better adapted to the American style of furnishing. Still, the fireplace often retained its characteristic eliptical opening.

New Mexico architecture prior to the mid-19th century — with the exception of Catholic missions and Indian religious structures — had been exclusively domestic. Merchants and tradesmen did business from rooms in the house; even the Palace of the Governors had been both residence and political headquarters for 250 years. The Anglo sensibility regarding business and commerce now demanded something else. So, with the other Eastern elements of the style, came new types of buildings expressly for commerce, industry and institutional use. Though few of the earliest examples remain,

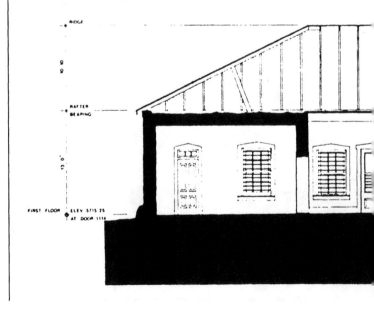

they were usually built with decorative elements of Greek-Territorial inspiration.

From a general survey of existing Territorial period buildings, there is little evidence to suggest that there was any noticeable advance in energy-conserving building technology during the period, or that glass was used in conjunction with passive solar ideas. Except in the case of earlier, south-preferred Indian and Spanish construction which was later fitted with windows, few buildings show any preference toward location of glass for solar gain. By and large, windows were just as likely to appear on east, west and north walls. This may in part have had to do with the wider plans and desire for lighting rooms which did not face south. If not an erosion of traditional conserving patterns, it at least represents a failure to capitalize on the potentials of the new materials for passive solar heating.

The Stone Warehouse, in Santa Fe, is one of the earliest surviving structures built during the Territorial period expressly for commerce and trade. The large glass windows — very large for their time — face the street to the east, not the winter sun to the south.

Interior section of the Tunsdall Store in Lincoln, New Mexico. Note the localized symmetries of the various rooms (similar to Territorial modifications to the Palace of the Governors), and the manner in which a wood-truss roof is added over an earth roof in particular rooms. (Architect's Atelier, for the Museum of New Mexico, State Monuments Division)

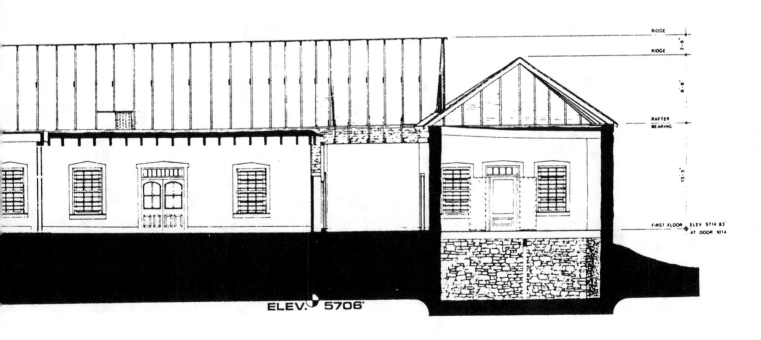

RIDGE
RIDGE
RAFTER BEARING
FIRST FLOOR   ELEV 5714 83' AT DOOR 101A
ELEV. 5706'

The Quartermaster's Headquarters at Fort Union was a classic example of the Greek Revival as applied to regional adobe buildings; few buildings of comparable design quality have been built since, though the style is still popular over 100 years later.

The row of Officer's Quarters at Fort Union. Such confident monumentality must have asserted a reassuring image of 'civility' to the Santa Fe Trailweary pioneer (U.S. Army Signal Corps. Museum of New Mexico Photo Archives)

FORT UNION

The quintessential expression of Territorial architecture may have been found at Fort Union, where buildings, both individually and in overall ensemble, presented an almost ideal manifestation of American Neo-classicism. The fort was abandoned in 1891, and very little remains today, due to natural deterioration and salvage for other construction; but sufficient documenation exists to give a good idea of what it was like:

After New Mexico became U.S. territory, the Army set up its department headquarters and principal supply depot at Fort Marcy in Santa Fe. This arrangement proved unsatisfactory, and in April 1851 Lt. Col. Edwin Sumner was ordered to take command of the defenses of New Mexico and 'revise the whole system of defense.' One of his first acts was to establish Fort Union to which he moved the headquarters and depot in August. Thus he got the soldiers close to the Indians — one of the main reasons Federal troops were in New Mexico — and away

The University of Virginia campus, designed by Thomas Jefferson, employed a continuous colonnade with pedimented pavillions to delineate a confined quadrangle. It is still one of the pinnacles of American urban design. Though the Fort Union colonnade is not continuous, the intent and scale are similar.

from Santa Fe, 'that sink of vice and extravagance.' (Excerpt from Fort Union, a pamphlet published by the National Park Service U.S. Department of the Interior, GPO 1977.)

First, a log fort, and during the Civil War, a second star-shaped earth fort were built near the site, along the Santa Fe Trail. After New Mexico was secured in the bonds of the Union in 1862, work was begun on the new compound, consisting of a military post, supply depot and hospital. It was a grand notion, (and was sharply criticized in some official quarters for its extravagance). An image of order, strength, and moral purity was desired, and it was realized in Doric Greek.

As Americans came west over the Santa Fe Trail in an increasing surge, killing off the Plains Indians' game and homesteading their land, the native people rebelled. Fort Union was established as headquarters from which to dispense supplies, protect the Trail and settle the "Indian problem" once and for all. This it did by the 1880s, and like most forts of its day, it was sufficiently overwhelming to do so without defensive walls. It was apparent that the U.S. military meant business.

Fort Union was sited on a wide, windswept plain at the foot of the Sangre de Cristo Mountains, near the junction of the Mountain Branch and Cimarron Cutoff of the Santa Fe Trail. Relatively little, in terms of overall planning and architecture, appears to have been done in response to the challenge of the rather harsh clmate. The scale of things and separation of buildings would not have done much to protect from winds out of the mountain west; and to prevailing winter northerners, it was wide open. Colonnades were far less than optimal in their provision for summer shade. Windows were largest on the northeast and respond equally, north and south, to the centralized floor plans. Chimneys, at least, were on the interior of the building for greater heating efficiency.

Major buildings were formally arrayed in a great row facing onto the parade ground. Functionary buildings were generally more in the tradition of prevailing regional vernacular, less formally dressed, and across the field. Officer's quarters and some of the other major buildings had Greek porticos, facing northeast, forming a great, discontinuously colonnaded elevation. With the dramatic backdrop of the Sangre de Cristos, it must

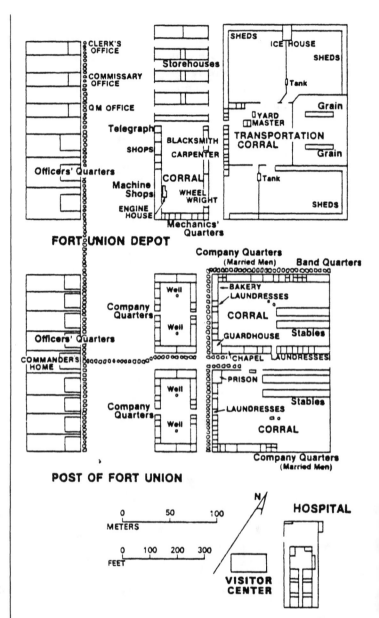

Ground plan of Fort Union, covering about 35 acres. There is little topographic mandate for the overall orientation of the complex; it is also not particularly well sited against the winds, or for solar exposure. Could it be that the principal elevations of the most formal buildings (the Officer's Quarters, at the left) are intended to face the mecca of territorial power, Washington, D.C.? (National Park Service, U.S. Department of the Interior)

Shutters on the more commodious buildings at Fort Union enhance their formal composition, while allowing for more effective climate control. (Museum of New Mexico Photo Archives)

have looked enormously civilized in 1865, and no doubt, would have been very reassuring to the trail-weary pioneer. And very forbidding to the nomadic Indians. A similarity to Thomas Jefferson's colonnaded quadrangle at the University of Virginia is not beyond imagination. (Indeed, physical separation of the more important, formal buildings was a significant departure from the old standard of fortified enclosure, and could be interpreted as a kind of deliberate thumbing-of-noses, from a position of overwhelming authority.)

The indigenous architecture of New Mexico lent itself quite handsomely to the new style. With simple lumber, Doric was easier to build than, say, Corinthian or Queen Anne. The structural requirements of adobe walls limited the size and placement of

openings to a degree quite compatible with the scale relationship of surface-and-opening in classical architecture: there was always a lot of surface around doors and windows, enhancing their quality of monumentality.

All in all, the Territorial style produced a remarkable impact on the development of New Mexico's architecture. It is still in widespread use in Revival form, with commercial and governmental buildings in particular. Square corners and standard windows render it more economical than the voluptuously contoured (when well done), highly romantic Pueblo-Spanish Revival. Though it would be difficult to find any indigenous architecture which has not, at some time, been visited by the neo-Greek, it seems to this writer that there is no more handsome, regionally adapted Neoclassicism to be found anywhere.

*A preeminently mad array of Steamboat Gothic exuberances, applied to a Western frontier farmhouse.
(Museum of New Mexico Photo Archives)*

CHAPTER 4
RAILROAD STYLES

This history focuses on regional, largely adobe styles, which form the backbone of New Mexico's architectural heritage. However, there are also many buildings in the state which are similar in style and technology to those found in any Eastern or Midwestern town; this survey would not be complete without some mention of their contribution to the evolution of regional tastes and building technology. Representing a wide range of eclectic and revival movements of the late 19th and early 20th centuries, they have been collectively identified here as the Railroad Styles. Like the Santa Fe Trail and its Territorial style before them, it was the railroad which formed the technical and cultural artery for their introduction in New Mexico.

When the railroad arrived in New Mexico — Raton and Las Vegas in 1879 and Santa Fe and Albuquerque in 1880 — an economical high-speed bridge to Eastern goods and ideas was opened. As train routes pushed westward in the late 1800s, the Santa Fe Trail shrank accordingly until it was gone altogether. No longer were builders limited by what could be locally procured or hauled by wagon over the Trail.

Things that were vogue in the East became vogue in New Mexico, only later. People, materials, technology and stylistic trends took some time to get here, but when they did, they made an indelible impact. Like Denver in the same period, Las Vegas, the eastern-most center on the railroad, quickly developed a very Midwestern appearance in its downtown business area, albeit around an earlier Mexican period plaza which adapted quite neatly into a more American town square. Las Vegas still has the best collection

45

In Las Vegas (New Mexico, not Nevada), the Plaza Hotel was the sumptuous new Queen of the west. The huge broken-and-scrolled pediment — artfully conceived for its time and place — was a beacon of civility in a town which had seen wagon trains only a year or so eariler.

of 19th century commercial buldings to be found in the state.

Almost every eclectic, romantic and revival style of the late Victorian period can be found in New Mexico; sometimes they are quite "pure" in their rendition, but more often, are mutated by lack of exactly the right trimmings and, of course, the rational and aesthetic influence of traditional native construction. Just the same, most of the extant historic buildings here, which are generally seen as regional, incorporate elements borrowed from non-indigenous or non-period sources. Selenite windows are seldom seen in the Indian pueblos now; Spanish Colonial period houses which survive often have Territorial doors and windows: buildings which are ostensibly Territorial frequently have Victorian windows; and a floor plan such as Taos Pueblo would be unthinkable in a Pueblo Revival house of the 1930s, though the overall visual intent is similar.

The Palace of the Governors is a large but typical example of this kind of layering; though the building looks more or less plausible as historic architecture today, actually it includes a Spanish Colonial shell, Territorial Greek Revival windows and doors, some Victorian interior trim and a Spanish Colonial Revival colonnaded portal. Somehow, it succeeds in coming full circle, over 300 years of evolution, to some sort of statement on the original theme. This free, adaptive use of style and technology is a motif which runs all through New Mexico's architectural history.

Among the smorgasbord of imported styles which arrived with the railroad were Gothic and Romanesque Revivals, Italiannate Bracketted Victorian, Queen Anne, Second Empire Mansard, Greek and Georgian

In Raton, a stripped-down version of the Romanesque Revival is visited in this stalwart commercial building, fronting on the trainyard itself.

Commercial buildings in major railroad towns were among the first to proudly state their new sophistication in styles and materials, including the cast iron and pressed metal seen here.

Revivals, Columbian Exposition Neoclassic, the gambrel-roofed Dutch Hudson River Style, the Prairie Style and American Craftsman, and from the West, Mission and Spanish Baroque Revival and, of course, the Bungalow. In short, just about anything one could find elsewhere, only less of it.

This bewildering array of styles is mentioned only briefly here, and is seldom referenced in Part II, because the various styles are covered in history and preservation literature elsewhere, and because there are relatively few examples of each to be found in New Mexico. For instance, there are probably no more than four really noteworthy examples

of Queen Anne in the entire state.

In terms of conservation technology, the slurry of styles which followed the railroad are probably not very distinguished. If anything, a new access to resources and an ethic of consumption tended to erode the native tradition of conservation. Certainly there were significant advances in building technology, permanence and comfort, such as the pitched metal roof. It kept the water off the walls far more effectively than a flat mud roof; it was cheaper, easier to install, and lasted longer than the board and batten wood roof, and it had the added benefit of an enclosed, insulating air space which could double as storage. Obviously, it caught on because it worked.

Though later buildings of the railroad era tended more and more to be built of wood

The Francisca Hinojos house, on Palace Avenue in Santa Fe, carries the mark of French artisans, brought to New Mexico from Louisiana by Archbishop Lamy to build the Cathedral. (Karl Kernberger, Museum of New Mexico Photo Archives)

frame and other low-mass materials, earlier examples, of necessity, were often built of adobe, with the stylistic reference material applied, much as it had been done in the preceding Territorial period.

A good example of this approach is the Mills-Clegg house in Springer, built in 1880 — one year after the railroad's arrival to northeastern New Mexico. This comfortable mansion featured a handsome blend of styles, varying from Territorial in pedimented doors and windows, and Queen Anne in porch woodwork, to Second Empire Mansard in

This historic photograph of the Leandro Martinez house suggests that the Carpenter Gothic trim was a later addition to a more classically Territorial building. The structure is now entirely gone. (Museum of New Mexico Photo Archives)

The Carpenter Gothic trim on the porch of the Leandro Martinez house in Ranchitos de Taos.

Detail of the porch and ballustrade, Mills-Clegg house, Springer.

North porch of the Mills-Clegg house in Springer. All of this High Style, and adobe too!

massing and roof treatment. The whole ensemble might have seemed a trifle bizarre by then-current Eastern standards, but it was still something of a phenomenon on the frontier plains, of which it commanded an impressive view.

What seems especially interesting about the Mills-Clegg house is its melding of traditional (real adobe) construction, solar considerations and its high-style overlay. The shell of the house is formed of massive adobe walls, set on stone footings. While few windows appear on the north elevation, they are numerous on the south, suggesting at least, a coherently planned solar exposure. Operating double-hung windows are mounted on both the interior and exterior faces of the two-foot thick walls, creating very convenient (if expensive) insulating windows, with limitless ventilation possibilities. The porch, which

originally ran around the entire perimeter of the building (somewhat in the manner of Steamboat Gothic, or the plantation houses of the Deep South) was deeper on the west and east, where summer shading would be desired, and more shallow on the south, affording winter solar gain on the large windows and adobe mass walls.

The combination of adobe construction and more glamorous appearance was rather eloquently expressed in Huning Castle, where it was, quite literally, a veneer. Built in Albuquerque in 1881 (and demolished in 1955), the house was rendered in a fashion resembling a medieval Italian villa which has received a serious overhaul during the Renaissance: Victorian Italiannate Bracketted. It was considered to be the most gracious house in the Territory. Inside the wood cladding, which produced the formal effect, were massive

More serious still, an elaborate porch applied to the spare, adobe, flat-roofed envelope of a house in Galisteo New Mexico. (New Mexico Office of Historic Preservation)

West porch or the Mills-Clegg house — which is wider than those of the north and south, though continuous with them — providing deep summer shade on both floors. (Arthur Lazar)

North elevation of the Mills-Clegg house. The south elevation is similar, but includes twice as many windows. (Historic American Buildings Survey)

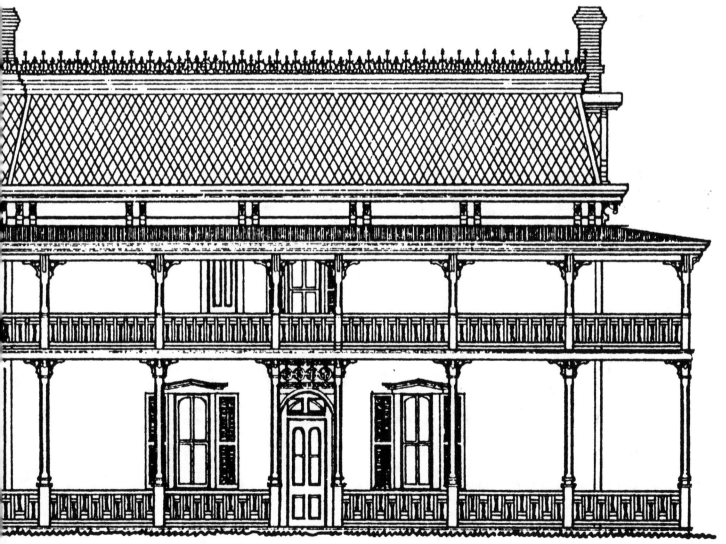

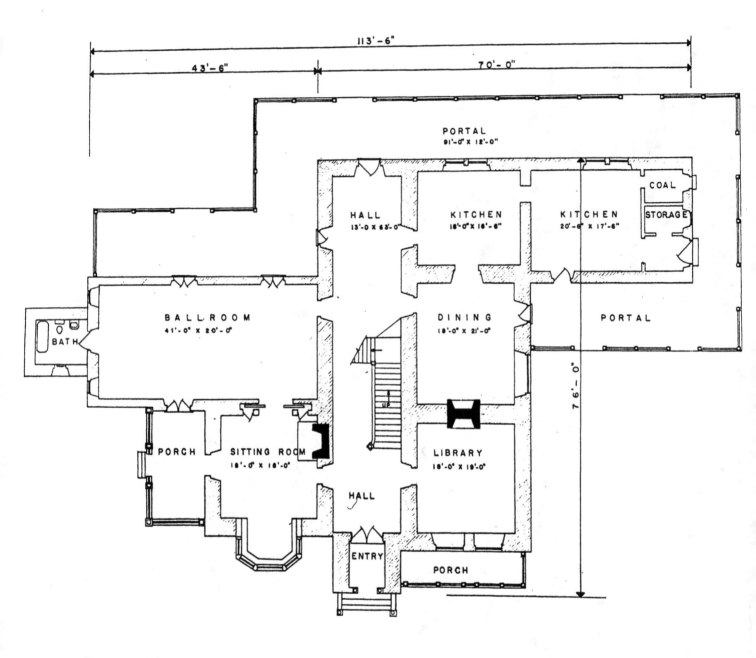

PORTAL
91'-0" X 12'-0"

HALL
13'-0 X 63'-0"

KITCHEN
18'-0" X 16'-6"

KITCHEN
20'-6" X 17'-6"

COAL

STORAGE

BALLROOM
41'-0" X 20'-0"

BATH

DINING
18'-0" X 21'-0"

PORTAL

PORCH

SITTING ROOM
18'-0" X 18'-0"

LIBRARY
18'-0" X 19'-0"

HALL

ENTRY

PORCH

113'-6"

43'-6"

70'-0"

76'-0"

walls of adobe. One suspects that as sawn wood was available, it was the known comfort of adobe in this climate which determined this curious structural approach. The beneficial effect of the thermal mass of adobe was preserved from indigenous practice, while the wood cladding and its heavily encrusted veneer decoration lent all the style anyone could want, and likely reduced maintenance and enhanced insulation somewhat. It did however, remove the dark earth from the direct benefit of winter solar absorption.

Huning Castle — reputedly the fanciest house in the Territory — was built in Albuquerque in 1881. It was demolished in 1955.

Its rather unorthodox construction featured massive adobe walls, entirely encased within a highly-detailed wood veneer! The intentions behind this somewhat bizarre construction are not known (to the author, at least), but might have had something to do with the superior water-shedding properties of wood, combined with the known comfort of indigenous earth buildings.

In this first floor plan, note the extensive, often 'wraparound' porches (similar to the Mills-Clegg house of the same period), and the provision of cross-ventilation for most of the rooms. (Museum of New Mexico Photo Archives)

Past its heyday (and shortly before the wrecking ball), extravagant Italianate details are still evident. (Museum of New Mexico Photo Archives)

The entrance facade of Huning Castle reveals an earnest homage to the Victorian Italianate Bracketed Style, as seen in fashionable houses of the contemporary East. However, certain provincial clumsiness is sometimes apparent, such as in the flat triangular pediment above the second story windows, to the right: perhaps a tongue-in-cheek statement on the (by then) banalities of the Territorial style which had preceded it. (Museum of New Mexico Photo Archives)

Interior view of the art gallery of the Dorsey Mansion. Though this historic photograph was taken after Dorsey sold the property, some of the furnishings are probably original — including perhaps the paintings, collected in Europe during his travels there. (Roe Seward collection, Raton, New Mexico.)

THE DORSEY MANSION

Another good example of early Railroad period construction with more than a little reference to regional antecedents is the Dorsey Mansion, on the northeastern plains between Springer and Clayton. It is certainly one of the most unusual if not outrageous episodes in all of New Mexico's architectural and political history. While it is not our immediate purpose to examine the built artifact in terms of Senator-and-cattle-baron Stephen W. Dorsey's personal career (recounted with great humor and insight in Thomas Caperton's *Rogue! Being an Account of the Life and High Times of Stephen W. Dorsey*), the property is noteworthy overall for its ingenious energy considerations. Notwithstanding a scale of indulgence, such as ducting water from a spring several miles away to fill a vast swimming pool – with three islands, Stephen Dorsey's elaborate fantasy is an interesting example of rural, low-tech, integrated design (In fact, not every resource was optimized, however: this piped-in stream might have been used as a source of hydroelectric power, but it was brought in over miles of poles instead.)

The Dorsey mansion began in 1878 as a rather formal, deluxe log house, vaguely Georgian in massing. In 1886, only eight years later, and shortly after the arrival of the railroad (by which time the owner's tastes had been transformed by what was then considered fashionable in the East), a castleated Romanesque Revival sandstone wing was added to the east. Slammed directly alongside one another, with a continuous porch at least inferring unity — the aesthetic, technical, and underlying social dialogue between these two structures paints a vivid, even racy, image of power on the late 19th century frontier.

The log house seems a natural expression of existing indigenous rural technology, albeit with a considerable comfort: pleasing, direct and sincere. A masterfully executed stone chimney flanks the west end, and despite the failure of second-story and dormer windows to align vertically with those so eloquently spaced and generously proportioned on the ground floor, the entire facade pulls together in a pleasantly rusticated formality.

The later sandstone addition is a perfect example of the infusion of Eastern materials and tastes, suddenly bestowed upon these remote places by the railroad. Though it might have been right at home in the best neighborhoods in 1880s Philadelphia, isolated on its windswept plain, beneath the arid mesas, it seems a flamboyant fantasy: complete with portrait busts of the owner and his wife, and gargoyle rain spouts in the form of Dorsey's worst enemy — President

Exterior view of the Dorsey Mansion with the earlier log section at left. The later sandstone addition boasts the somewhat rustified gentility of robber-baron Eastern tastes transposed onto the Western frontier — including gargoyle waterspouts in the visage of President Arthur, and portrait 'medallions' of Dorsey and his family. (LeRoy D. Maloney, Museum of New Mexico Photo Archives)

Chester A. Arthur.

In addition to the requisite entertaining rooms (and did Dorsey entertain!), the first floor features a 800 square foot art gallery, contained like a vault on the interior of the plan, and lit by an open-truss skylighted roof. All principal rooms are oriented to the east and south (preferred solar exposures), including 10 second-floor bedrooms, with a single-loaded corridor to buffer the temperature extremes of north and western exposures.

In both the log and stone sections of the house, the advantages of heavy mass material have been exploited. Log had been used as a building material for at least 100 years in the region, and it must have appealed to Dorsey's sense of regionalized romanticism, even though there wasn't a logable tree within

though there wasn't a logable tree within sight. In addition, its good insulating qualities mean that once warm air generated inside a tight log building, it stays there; likewise, it keeps the summer heat out. Stone, also an indigenous building material, has somewhat inferior insulating capabilities, but its high mass is able to collect and store heat, transmitting and radiating it slowly into the interior. (It would be interesting to moniter the two sections of Dorsey for comparison of their ambient, unassisted temperature variants.) The high pitched roofs on both sections provide an insulating attic space, and rain gutters are arranged to conduct water to a cistern located in the northwest interior corner of the L-shaped plan.

The Dorsey mansion was the seat of an empire which, at one time, claimed (despite considerable dispute) over 200 square miles. Dorsey's parties were legendary. He once reportedly imported an entire chorus line from Kansas City to entertain guests, while his wife was away. To flesh out the amenities of such a spread, the property also included — in addition to the huge artificial pond — several features which show further attention to conservation (it must have been essential in so remote a location). First and foremost, the property contained what the author suspects was probably the first passive solar greenhouse in the Southwest. It was built to the southeast of the main house, partially sunk into the ground, with massive stone east, west and north walls, and a south-sloping glass roof and glass south wall. A stroke of pragmatic genius: back-up heat was provided by the smoke house which was built adjacent to the east.

In siting, the house occupies one of the only semi-protected areas on a wide plain (which probably, then, had a good deal more grass). Mesas to the north and west provide some shelter from fierce winter winds. Extensive landscaping to the south and west, with formal gardens, paths, fountains, and the lake of course — with three islands and one gazebo — are perfectly sited so that dry summer winds, blowing in around the end of the mesa, may take advantage of the massive evaporation of this 'park' to cool the house. There was also a root cellar, buried near water and in the shade of an ancient cottonwood. A carriage house and servants' quarters to the north were also aligned on the east-west axis, with large openings to the south.

The floor plans show the major rooms in two wings; on the second floor, a single-loaded corridor orients all bedrooms to the south or east. (Conron and Lent, Architects, for the Museum of New Mexico, State Monuments Division)

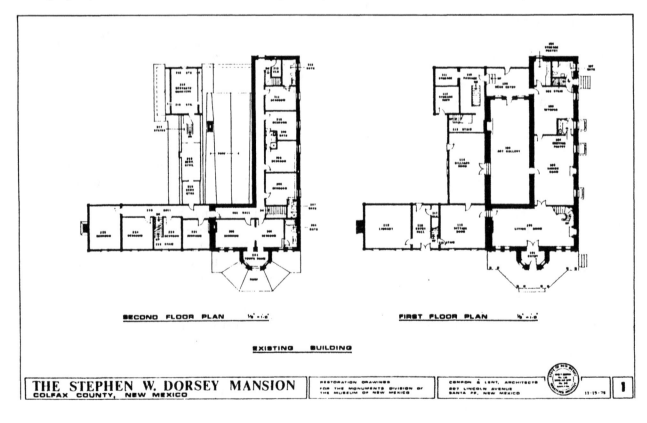

SECOND FLOOR PLAN

FIRST FLOOR PLAN

EXISTING BUILDING

THE STEPHEN W. DORSEY MANSION
COLFAX COUNTY, NEW MEXICO

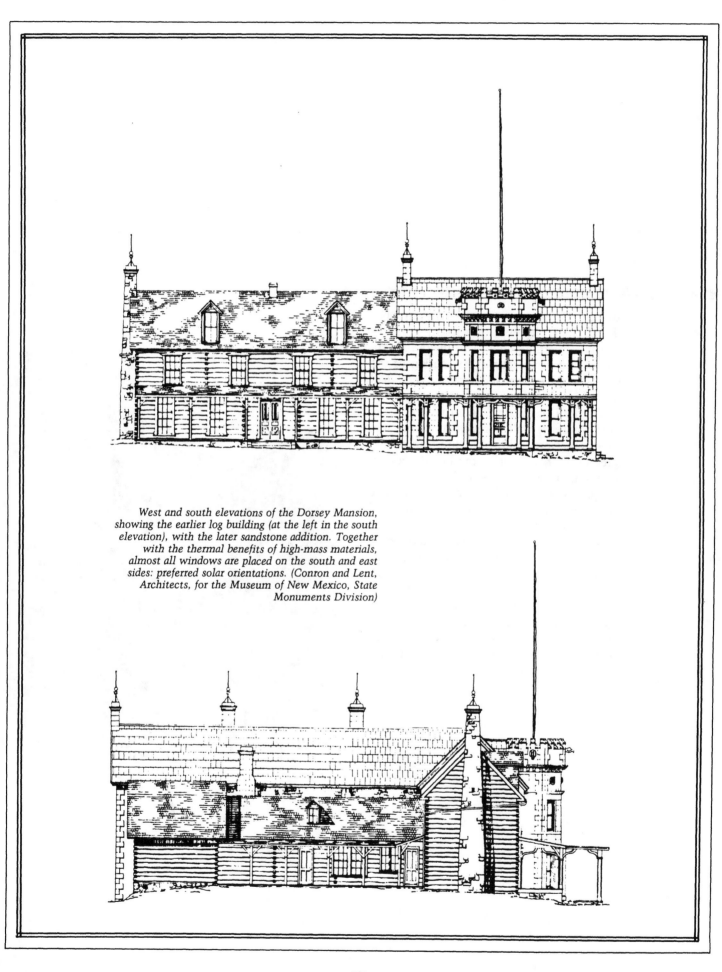

West and south elevations of the Dorsey Mansion, showing the earlier log building (at the left in the south elevation), with the later sandstone addition. Together with the thermal benefits of high-mass materials, almost all windows are placed on the south and east sides: preferred solar orientations. (Conron and Lent, Architects, for the Museum of New Mexico, State Monuments Division)

While the Dorsey mansion was anything but self-sufficient, its use of certain resource potentials is impressive. The overall socio-political and architectural distinction of the property suggests that it deserves a good deal more attention.

The Railroad period, like the Territorial period before it, isn't noteworthy for its success in creating buildings exhibiting a high degree of energy — or in the broader arena, resource consciousness — unlike the Indian and Spanish eras which preceded them. The Mills-Clegg house, Huning Castle and Dorsey mansion are all exceptions, however instructive. They all, also, date from relatively early in the railroad era. Later, the American abundance-waste syndrome seems to supersede. Though indigenous concepts of conservation were fading fast from the scene, a growing appreciation for the nature of regional style — if not sensibility — appeared just in time to save at least the 'look' native to the place: the Revival Styles.

Late 19th century affluence is evident in this house in Tierra Amarilla. The square plan reflects the influence of Territorial and Railroad-Victorian ideas, and the availability of milled lumber, while the porch roof — continuous with the main roof — is particular to this locality. It may represent the practical wisdom of folk tradition in how to get lots of snow off the roof.

CHAPTER 5

MOUNTAIN GABLED STYLES

Much of the historic architecture of New Mexico sports elements of non-regional style absorbed into a native vocabulary as witnessed in the Territorial and Railroad periods. After the railroad, a lot of the architecture was very eclectic in character, varying widely within close proximity. However, in certain concentrated areas — isolated mountain valleys, in particular — some popular recipes became so established as to emerge as sub-regional styles in their own right.

A formula we might call the Mountain Gabled style is a case in point. Part Spanish-Mexican, part Territorial and part Railroad, it is certainly eclectic, if uncomplicated. The style derives a great deal of its elegance from this spare simplicity, like the decorated shed in modern architectural terms. "Mountain Gabled" is a kind of collective term for a group of related forms. In fact, not all of its buildings are seen in the mountains, nor do all of them have gables; it seems, however, like a reasonable label for a loosely identifiable family. Some may consider this type of building simply a rural, pitched-roof branch of the Territorial, but to the author, its easy incorporation of a variety of non-Greek elements seems to suggest a separate sub-species.

There are variations on the theme, but the identifying characteristics are: single file plans (straight, L, or U) with adobe walls and plaster (or occasionally later, cement stucco) (Spanish-Mexican); Neo-Greek door and window casings, often with simple pediments, usually painted white, or sometimes blue or other colors (Territorial); and high-pitched metal roofs with overhanging eaves (introduced in the Territorial era, but popularized later in rural areas (Railroad period).

Certain regional sub-themes are also present within the style. Around Tierra Amarilla, in the Chama River Valley, many later buildings have deeper, square plans. Roofs are massive corrugated metal constructions (not unlike the thatch of traditional Japanese farm houses) and their line is often continued directly into a long porch roof. Penasco and other northern areas sometimes feature portales with hardcarved or machine-turned columns, often painted in contrasting bright colors; and scrolled metal ridge finials appear around Belen, to the south — both features vaguely Queen Anne in flavor. Double-hung windows, with large 2-over-2 lights (Victorian and not Territorial), are also common elsewhere.

The degree of Mountain Gabled style's popularity in certain areas might be easily explained in terms of its simple, direct beauty and classic proportion. However, its widespread adaptation is probably due as much to function as to aesthetics: each of the three key elements represent specific advantages in building technology. First, there is a high-mass Spanish adobe shell; then windows and doors appear, enhancing lighting and ventilation; then the railroad provided an inexpensive and durable roofing material in sheet metal: much more effective than the earlier flat earth roofs in shedding water. Without further elaboration or frills, the style is fully-formulated and complete.

Access to the new seems to have caused loss of contact with energy conserving native traditions during much of the southwest's architectural history. The Mountain Gabled style is a notable exception. Surviving well into the 20th century— it finally achieved its own modest revival in the 1970 and 80s— the style incorporated only essential technical improvements over previous solutions.

In terms of energy and thermal performance, the Mountain Gabled style is best represented by a broad sample profile, rather than by individual buildings, though there may be some distinguished examples. Architectural style is intrinsically understated and individual buildings do not cry out to be noticed; this may be a reflection of the conservative nature of society in rural Spanish areas. Large

Rancho de Chimayo, in northern New Mexico. This is a good example of what we have called here the Mountain Gabled style. Essentially, there seem to be three typical ingredients: a single-file Spanish Colonial style adobe house; Territorial or other late-19th century windows and doors; and a high pitched roof — this one of characteristic corrugated metal, painted in dark red, artfully completing the harmonious ensemble of brown white, and red. This old Spanish house, owned by Arturo Jaramillo, is now a restaurant.

or small, the overall appearance of the structures, mostly houses, is similar, if differently seasoned.

This makes a rather homogenous atmosphere in some mountain areas, like Penasco. One can see ways in which a whole local population viewed its natural ecology and developed a pervasive vernacular language to

Three views of a farmhouse near Los Brazos, in the Chama River highlands. These buildings seem to project a very sincere charm, and show the subtle localized variation with which the Mountain Gabled architectural formula is often imbued.

Shallow porches wrap the east and south sides, and dormer windows suggest that the second floor was occupied. (Note, also, that chimneys are on the interior of the building — not on end gable walls — optimizing the use of heat stored in their large mass.)

Woodwork on the porch, like other buildings in the Tierra Amarilla area of northern New Mexico, is inflected with 19th century eclecticism: double-hung windows, Queen Anne turned columns, and carpenter scrollwork brackets.

South end of the main house, well shed, and barn. The ensemble of architectural form is perfectly maintained. Simple but finesseful detailing of the house — such as the ridge finial lightning rods — lend it distinction as the residence.

respond to local conditions. Maybe evidence of the hands of local building specialists and craftsmen is felt as well. But the architecture unity of these areas changed with time.

To illustrate this point, a 'windshield survey' was made of the Penasco valley east and upstream from the town of Penasco for a distance of 10 kilometers. The valley contains traditional farmlands with structures dating from the early 19th century up to the present. With building orientation, in particular, an evolution (or devolution) in prevailing strategy seems to become apparent.

The 121 houses counted in the valley are broken down into three general periods of construction, as suggested by their materials, technology and configuration. The dates are rough, but generally there were approximately 59 (49%) in the rural 19th century single-file mode. These usually have pitched metal roofs, though a few still show the flat earth roof. The next period — with wide, more squarish plans encouraged by sawn lumber

The dormer-porch reveals the inference of Queen Anne, simplified by provincial practicality and limited materials.

Porch detail from the same house in Tierra Amarilla. Store-bought columns attest to the prosperity of the owners.

Porch post in Tierra Amarilla. For most buildings, handmade renditions of the column and capital ensemble were still the rule of the day.

A single-file adobe hacienda, in Tierra Amarilla. The keynote features of the Mountain Gabled style are seen in this large house in a once-prosperous mining area.

Though most aspects of the design reflect late 19th century tastes and materials, the plazuela-type plan represents much earlier Spanish traditions.

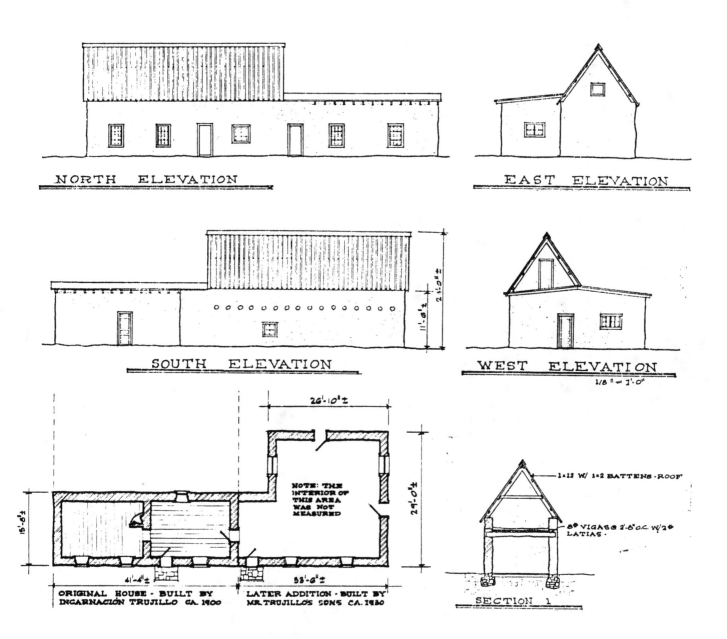

NORTH ELEVATION

EAST ELEVATION

SOUTH ELEVATION

WEST ELEVATION

1/8" = 1'.0"

26'-10"±

29'-0"±

NOTE: THE
INTERIOR OF
THIS AREA
WAS NOT
MEASURED

15'-8"±

41'-4"±   52'-6"±

ORIGINAL HOUSE - BUILT BY   LATER ADDITION - BUILT BY
INCARNACIÓN TRUJILLO CA. 1900   MR. TRUJILLO'S SONS CA. 1930

1x12 W/ 1x2 BATTENS · ROOF

8" VIGAS@ 2'-6" O.C. W/2"
LATIAS.

SECTION 1

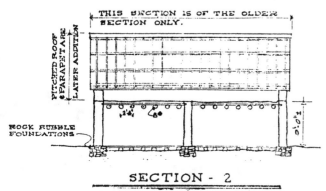

THIS SECTION IS OF THE OLDER
SECTION ONLY.

PITCHED ROOF
& PARAPET ARE
LATER ADDITION

ROCK RUBBLE
FOUNDATIONS

SECTION - 2

The Incarnacion Trujillo house in Talpa, near Taos, built around 1900, the very high-pitched roof — of lapped-board sheathing, covering a flat roof of conventional viga-and-latilla construction — shows how long traditional construction techniques lasted in remote areas. (Fort Burgwin Research Center, Southern Methodist University)

The Robert Love house in Tesuque, northern New Mexico, built by Betty Stewart in the early 1970s. The artful simplicity — and practical advantages — of the Mountain Gabled style are contributing to its rediscovery among a sophisticated audience today: regionalism in the less-glamorous trappings of an adaptive, eclectic vernacular.

Three typical houses of the Penasco Valley, in northern New Mexico. First, a single-file east-west adobe house of the Spanish Colonial period, retrofitted with a post 1880 pitched metal roof. Second, an L-shaped house, with a secondary wing to the southwest, and a more complex gable-on-hip roof. Third, the typical early 20th century square plan, with pyramidal metal roof. These styles prevailed until after World War II, at which time industrialized housing and mobile homes supersede them in popularity.

and sheet metal roofing materials — from late in the 19th century until about 1945, numbers 40 (33%). Many of these are made of adobe, though few probably have a flat earth roof beneath the pitched one. The third group, representing the arrival of industrialized housing after World War II — in the form of mobile homes and prefabs, or buildings which look a lot like them — numbers 22 (18%). These are often found as structures adjacent to older buildings, probably built as houses for grown children and their families.

These 121 houses are shown on the accompanying chart, as they break down into orientation categories for each period. From the mid-1950s on, no pattern was apparent, and for the first time, non-orthogonal siting becomes evident. (In other words, the east-west and north-south pattern of earlier construction finds diagonal orientation introduced, particularly with mobile homes, which could be viewed as 'temporary' though they seldom are.)

PERIOD	% OF TOTAL FROM PERIOD	PREDOMINANT EAST - WEST	PREDOMINANT NORTH - SOUTH	OTHER
1800 - 1910 SINGLE FILE ADOBE, EARTH OR PITCHED ROOF TOTAL NUMBER COUNTED: 59	65%	*(house diagrams)*		
	15%		*(house diagrams)*	
1910 - 1950 WIDER, DEEPER HOUSES, MOSTLY ADOBE; HIP METAL ROOF TOTAL NUMBER COUNTED: 40	55%	*(house diagrams)*		
	35%		*(house diagrams)*	
	10%			*(house diagrams)*
1950 - 1980 MOBILE HOMES MANUFACTURED HOUSING OR CONTEMPORARY RANCH STYLE TOTAL NUMBER COUNTED: 22	32%	*(house diagrams)*		
	41%		*(house diagrams)*	
	27%			*(house diagrams)*

This chart illustrates 121 houses in the upper Penasco Valley, as they break down into general periods of construction and orientation. The later one gets in the historic chronology, the less orientation-specific buildings tend to be.

OBSERVATIONS

The elevation of the Penasco Valley is about 7400 to 7600 feet above sea level and the heating season is about 7000 degree-days. Cooling in summer is not a serious problem but winters demand the maximizing of intrinsic site advantages to reduce the substantial heating requirement.

Houses are frequently cut into the south sloping grade down to the river. Many are entered on the north, with a more private, semi-enclosed space to the south.

The valley runs generally east and northeast. Though superior views might be seen toward the west, down the valley, older houses tend to be east-west axial in massing (an impressive 85%), oriented to face across the valley to the south.

Prevailing winds come up the valley from the west, so the significantly less popular north-south axis house would suffer more surface to heat loss. When an addition was made onto the predominant single-file east-west house, more often than not, it was made on the southwest: better to deflect the wind from the solar-absorbing south wall and outdoor living area.

The older the houses are, the more orientation-specific they tend to be. Each generation has increasingly eroded a once-strong pattern.

Interestingly, the early east-west pattern (with preferred southwest wing) can be seen in several other regions, while it is absent in others with very similar climate and site constraints, suggesting that the strength of local tradition and folk wisdom in construction varies considerably within a relatively small area. The Penasco Valley pattern is also pervasive in neighboring Las Trampas and across the Rio Grande at Chamita, near the site of the second Spanish Colonial settlement of San Gabriel de Yunque. However, just across La Junta Pass in the Sangre de Cristos, the region of Mora has a prevailing grid-like orthogonal orientation of buildings (n/s or e/w), but there appears to be no clear preference in direction. Again, in the central and southern portion of the state, towns such as Lincoln generally have east-west pattern, but others, such as Alamogordo do not.

The evidence of this Penasco Valley survey would suggest that, as resources became more accessible, people quickly learned to waste them. Fortunately for Penasco, an effective indigenous tradition still exists, in form and memory, to suggest appropriate and contextually relevant directions in future construction.

As passive solar architecture appears in a subsequent generation of forms, like it has in other areas of the state, the traditional east-west pattern will almost certainly be reinstated. Despite the romantic, perhaps even nostalgic appeal of the flat roof, its technical drawbacks — particularly in adobe construction — seem to be contributing to a revival of interest in pitched roofs. The classically pragmatic Mountan Gabled style's unassuming beauties are likely to be perpetuated.

CHAPTER 6
LOG CONSTRUCTION

Adzes or large, two-man saws were used to dress timbers to square shapes before the first sawmills were established. Mud was often applied over log to help seal against the weather. The use of solid log planking for roof/ceiling is somewhat uncommon, attesting to the local good availability of timber.

Holes sometimes appear in the end of the logs, and were used to attach ropes for hauling them down from the mountains, frequently some miles away. (Truman Matthews, Museum of New Mexico Photo Archives)

Most of the forests of the American Southwest are at elevations above 7000 feet, where short growing seasons have traditionally discouraged human settlement. The indigenous materials of more habitable lower elevations — adobe and stone — therefore prevail in historic buildings. Timber, which had to be hauled some distance, was used primarily for roof construction in the earlier more populated lower elevations. Though log buildings are fewer in number, they assume an important position in historic regional architecture, with each of the Southwest's three major cultures contributing to the development of technology and architectural style.

Timber was used in the construction of Indian pit houses at least as early as 300 AD. With the emergence of the prehistoric Puebloan culture, logs were used for the construction of flat roofs, but apparently not for the walls of houses. It seems that log walls were reserved for ancillary structures, like storage rooms and animal shelters. Navajo Indians, in the same region, later adapted something vaguely like the pit house into the traditional hogan, which at higher elevations often had walls of vertical or horizontal log. Spruce poles, of course, figured importantly in the mobile tepee structures of the nomadic Indian tribes on the eastern plains: a most economical and surprisingly comfortable architecture.

With Spanish settlement, log continued in use primarily for flat roof construction: the *vigas* which formed the major supporting beams. Where wood was employed in the construction of walls, Indian and early Spanish structures were usually of wattle and daub or *jacal*: a vertical stick or light pole network, horizontally laced with branches and covered

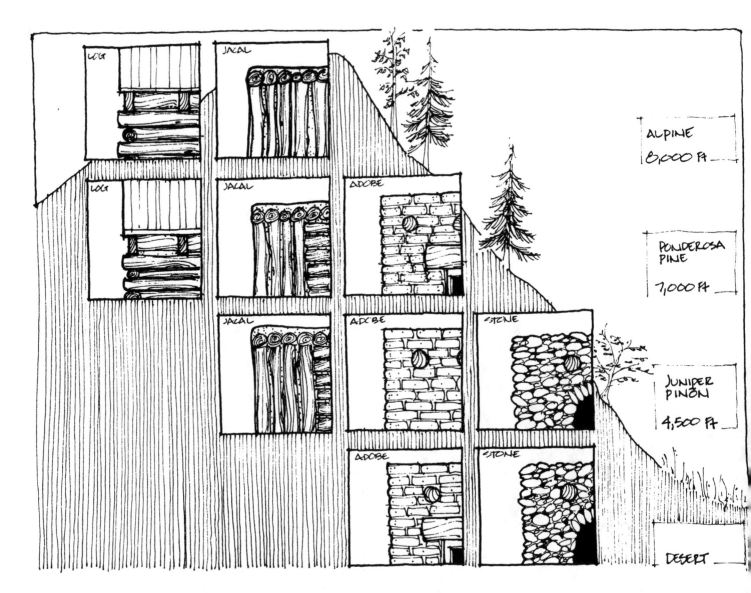

ALPINE
8,000 FT

PONDEROSA
PINE

7,000 FT

JUNIPER
PIÑON

4,500 FT

DESERT

with heavy mud (rather like today's reinforced concrete). The roof was flat and of timber, brush and mud. Later Spanish developments permitted by the increasing availability of metal tools in the 19th century, included a dressed-log structural system: heavy, upright members, set close together in a trench, and tied together at the top with a continuous notched log. The wall was chinked (filled between the cracks) and often plastered overall with mud, making the finished appearance almost indistinguishable from adobe-core walls. Erosion of aged plaster sometimes reveals a building of log, where adobe was assumed.

Horizontal log construction, with round or square-adzed timbers, and notched, overlapping corners, was popular in Hispanic mountain areas between the early 19th and early 20th centuries. Roofs on these buildings might be either flat, or later, pitched, with

Diagram showing typical building materials by altitude. Log is primarily limited to higher, more wooded elevations. (Adapted from Charles Gritzner, Pioneer America, 1974, Vol. 6, No. 1, p. 26)

rafters. Horizontal log construction was used for both houses and outbuildings. Among the surviving examples in highland regions many are in an advanced state of deterioration.

Heavy timber construction lost favor in the late 19th century, when sawn lumber became available, though sporadic resurgences are evident up to the present day. Log construction enjoyed something of a renaissance in the early 20th century — with buildings such as the El Tovar at the Grand Canyon — and in the 1920s and 30s, particularly in Depression-era public works projects intended to stimulate local economies. The WPA log and stone buildings in New Mexico's Hyde State Park are fine examples. Low-cost,

indigenous materials, and labor-intensive building techniques were the objectives, and were handsomely realized in structures of lasting durability and unpretentious style.

Certain highly localized applications of timber construction are also found. They exhibit their own brand of folk-ingenuity. Around Cuba, New Mexico, at the western base of the Jemez Mountains, and in Mora County, on the eastern slopes of the Sangre de Cristos, a form of construction popular in the 1930s and 40s involves an interesting hybrid of post-and-beam, frame, and rubble infill — not altogether unlike traditional European half-timber. A heavy, squared post and beam structure is erected, with vertical rough sawn studs set at about 2 feet on-center and alongside windows and doors. Horizontal lath strips are nailed on the interior and exterior, and the cavities are then filled with mud and rock rubble. The lath keeps it in place. Plaster could then be applied, though the bare construction is visible on the exterior of many buildings (appearing never to have been plastered) making for a fascinating striped pattern on the elevations. An over-hanging roof kept water off the walls, and should the mud wash out in areas, it would be apparent, and exposed for easy repair.

In Chama, near the continental divide, and the neighboring vicinity, a technique locally known as "cross-tie" construction was popular, also in the 1930s and 40s. This method involved laying up standard square railroad ties in horizontal log cabin fashion, alternating courses at the corners, but without the typical cantilevered ends of round-log construction. The construction was tied together by simply toe-nailing successive courses and corners together with large "lead head" spikes, also a railroad product. Very neat. Never mind that the timber segments were only about eight feet long: the flat ends were easily butted together and the module adapted reasonably to the location of door and window openings. As Chama was a booming lumber and railroad center, the technique was fast,

Three various uses of wood in native construction. First, a Navajo hogan built of round timbers; second, pine poles used as a portable structure for a tepee, used by the Indians of the eastern plains; third a composite structure, probably Spanish, using both jacal and vertical logs. (J. Iowa; William Henry Jackson, Museum of New Mexico Photo Archives; anonymous, Museum of New Mexico Photo Archives)

The Fuller Lodge, built for the Los Alamos Ranch School in 1927, shows the persistence of log construction into the 20th century. Designed more for ranchy atmosphere than for energy efficiency, the grand two-story portal faces toward an eastern view, rather than the southern sun.

Massive flanking stone chimneys, which were originally on the exterior of the building, have been brought into the interior by later additions to both ends, increasing their effective storage mass. Behind the portal is a fine, large two-story room. (T. Harmon Parkhurst, Museum of New Mexico Photo Archives)

East portal of the Fuller Lodge

70

cheap, durable, and somehow, symbolically appropriate.

Many buildings in Chama were constructed in this manner (and elsewhere in the region as well, where railroad lines were nearby), though they are usually plastered over to preserve the wood and stop air infiltration through the cracks — alleviating the need for careful chinking, as with round-log walls. With plaster, the buildings are hard to tell from adobe, except corners may be sharper and walls generally more plumb.

In both of these techniques — post-and-beam with rubble infill, and railroad cross-tie construction — locally available materials with high mass are used; and in the case of the all wood cross-tie walls, there are excellent insulative properties as well. As modern industrialized buildings have become increasingly dominant in these once-remote areas since the 1950s, these techniques have died out — though the cross-tie method would probably still prove to be a quick, relatively inexpensive and energy-effective way to built. It is interesting to note the time period of these populist vernacular approaches: while modern industrialized housing (using 2 x 4 balloon framing and so forth) was sweeping other areas of the nation in the 1940s, remote areas of the Southwest were still developing, and utilizing, ingenious, low-tech, energy-efficient building techniques. The pragmatic, provincial conserving spirit was still alive.

ENERGY AND THE LOG BUILDING

Generally, log buildings are found in areas of higher elevation, with more precipitation and stands of good timber nearby (and, of course, log buildings look more at home near trees than in the desert terrain of lower elevation). In terms of climatic response, not only does the higher precipitation of mountain regions make adobe less effective structurally and thermally (wet adobe in winter is both

A cross-tie building in Chama. This technique was occasionally practiced in various areas of the Southwest where the railroad was nearby to provide the materials.

Detail of a corner, showing the overlap of the short massive railroad ties, held together only by gravity and long nails.

Exposed lath of Southwestern 'half-timber' construction, such as one finds around Cuba, in northern New Mexico. The 1930s and 40s saw the use of milled-wood materials: perhaps an extension and adaptation of the regional tradition of jacal or 'wattle-and-daub.'

71

cold and slowly dissolving), but wood actually performs better for its cellular structure affords a better deterent to water and superior insulation for the colder climate. Just the same, the choice of log over adobe might represent a primarily aesthetic preference, such as architect Charles Whittlesey's rather curious house in Albuquerque (a more detailed analysis follows). In siting and execution, the region's log buildings often demonstrate simple considerations for comfort and energy efficiency, including solar orientation, south windows and north-side berming.

Preferred building sites in mountain regions tend toward clearings on south-facing slopes. One had only to observe a valley under a heavy winter snow cover to realize that a south slope melted much faster than a north slope. At Evergreen Valley Ranch, in the high-

Evergreen Valley Ranch outbuildings. These are grouped in a continuous row, built into the south slope so that the back wall is entirely buried.

The cross-axis pitched roof covers a subterranean root cellar, entered through the 'airlock' of the front room.

Main house at Evergreen Valley Ranch south patio terrace. Observing the situation and construction of older log buildings in the valley, the owner designed and built this energy-efficient structure in 1949. Note the simple and effective splayed angle of the west wing.

Because of its good insulating qualities, log was often employed by the Spaniards in the construction of storage buildings. These two examples — one partially buried and probably freeze-proof — are from Rancho de las Golondrinas.

lands of San Miguel County's Gallinas Canyon, several log structures dating back to the mid 1880s gave a 20th century builder design clues when he built his own log house in 1949 (not technically historic, but worth discussion just the same). The house sits in an exposed, south-sloping clearing, with deciduous trees for summer shade. Massing has been intelligently developed to provide a winter sun trap, with the west wing of the U-shaped plan splayed at an angle to catch winter morning sun, yet not shade the patio in the afternoon.

Few openings appear on the north wall. The pitched roof creates an insulating attic space, which is accessed outside from the gable end, as in traditional Spanish gable construction. Heat is chiefly provided by wood stoves rather than less-efficient fireplaces. The one main fireplace is located on the interior of the building, to utilize heat stored in the masonry mass. Outbuildings are cleverly grouped in a row, cut into the north bank at the rear of the house, and include a partially-buried greenhouse and a completely buried root cellar.

While most of the Southwest's historic and almost-historic log buildings are simple in nature — direct, unstylized and truly vernacular — occasionally log was employed on larger, more formal buildings, like the older section of the Dorsey Mansion (1878), the Charles Whittlesey house in Albuquerque (1903), the original buildings of the Museum of Northern Arizona in Flagstaff, and the Los Alamos Ranch School's Fuller Lodge (1927).

THE WHITTLESEY HOUSE

The Charles Whittlesey house in Albuquerque is an interesting, if not altogether typical, example of timber construction in the Southwest, particularly in light of its energy conserving design features. (Actually, it is not even the log building it appears to be; but its consideration seems more appropriate here than with the Railroad styles, of which it is, quite literally, a product.)

Charles Whittlesey was chief architect of hotels for the Atchison Topeka & Santa Fe Railroad at the turn of the century. The Santa Fe Railroad and its affiliate, the Harvey House chain of restaurants and hotels, were responsible for many fine buildings throughout the West, including the extraordinary El Tovar at the Grand Canyon, and the Alvarado Hotel in Albuquerque (demolished in 1970), both of which Whittlesey designed.

While handling El Tovar and other western assignments for the railroad, Whittlesey moved his family from Chicago to a house he designed in Albuquerque — on what was then a barren hilltop to the east of the city, in Huning Highlands. The Whittlesey House now presides over wooded Highland Park, and is still one of the more arresting architectural features in the city.

Whittlesey sold the house in 1908 when his work took him to Los Angeles, and it has had a fascinating history since, including a period in the 1930s when it served as a convalescent facility for Indians, who rested on its expansive verandas.

The building is styled along the lines of a Scandinavian villa, particularly in a cantilevered balcony (which has been removed; to the upper right in the elevation drawing,) and ballustrade ornamentation. It could be regarded as something of a folly, but it achieves a charming balance with more mainstream rural Western architecture of the period, especially in it low gable-on-hip east front

North elevation of the Whittlesey house, in which a Western ranch house or lodge aesthetic comingles with features of a Scandinavian Villa, particularly apparent on this elevation. Aside from its extreme curiosity in the natural landscape and architectural setting of Albuquerque, the design is particularly clever in its climate-moderating characteristics. (Greg Baczek)

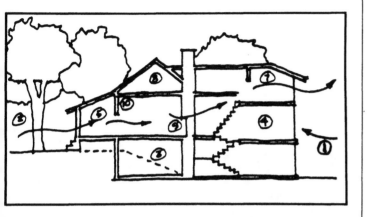

summer — because of several ingenious design features:

1. The western promontory of the site is broadly exposed to prevailing breezes in the summer, which aid in cooling (but can be a handicap in winter).

2. Deciduous trees were planted on the site, to shade the house on the east, south and west during the summer, while defoliating to allow the winter sun to enter.

3. Cut into the hillside, several subgrade rooms are well insulated by the earth itself.

4. Cross ventilation (with openings on at least two exposures) has been carefully planned for all rooms.

5. Deep verandas on the east and north shade the walls, and provide a cooler transition space for entering fresh air. They also reduce heat losses in winter by reducing the impact of the wind.

6. The veranda roof is cut away on the south side, leaving only an open-timbered structure to continue the architectural lines; deciduous vines provide summer shade, and losing their leaves in fall, winter sun enters to the large window.

7. Sleeping porches on the upper western levels provide shade on hot summer afternoons, and are exposed to cooling evening breezes.

8. Shallow pitched roofs, with attics, have been used to help insulate the house, most effectively the large east living room.

9. The massive stone fireplaces and chimney are on the interior of the building (though the architect might have been tempted to put them on exterior walls for visual effect.) On the interior, they store heat in the huge stone mass, and re-radiate it into the rooms, not to the outside.

10. The log facing slabs are between 2 and 4 inches thick on the interior and exterior, providing a degree of mass and some insulation. Building paper has been used under the slab sheathing to stop air infiltration, a typical problem in log buildings with deteriorated chinking.

Log construction continues to be popular today in higher-elevation, more wooded areas of the state, like Ruidoso. But more often than not, it is rendered in non-indigenous, slightly eccentric, 'Carpenter-gingerbread' style

elevation (which feels rather 'Texan'). It gets more Scandinavian as one moves around the north to the west. The house must have been an immensely curious sight when originally built, on a desert hilltop, "twenty miles from the nearest log." (Erna Fergusson, *Albuquerque.* Albuquerque: Merle Armitage Editions, 1947.) But today it looks comfortable in its wooded setting (albeit a man-made ecology,) though still quite out of character with the surrounding neighborhood's architectural context. Wonderfully so, for Huning Highlands possesses a diverse, if more predictable, eclecticism.

Conventional wisdom is that the house, and its adjacent stable buildings, are built of logs; this is obviously the architect's intent, for he has given considerable attention to the cosmetics of making it appear so. But while the verandas and various attachments are assertively log, the body of the house is actually conventional wood frame. Exterior and interior sheathing of sawn log slabs — only a few inches thick — create a successful illusion of solid log construction. (What a clever use of low-cost milling salvage material.) The effect is quite convincing — despite the 'logs' failure to always align at door and window jambs — due in large part to essential visual cues, like the actually attached cantilevered log corners, and the picturesque forked tree trunk columns supporting the veranda roof. Rough rockwork in foundation and chimney continues the woodsy theme.

In spite of lacking the mass of true log construction, this building is well-tempered to the climate — warm in winter and cool in

(vaguely reminiscent of the Swiss Alps) — a common fantasy exercised in the suburbanization of the Mountain West. Pre-cut component 'kits' have also contributed to the renewed popularity of log construction.

Whether rustic expressions like mountain barns, or more refined examples like the Fuller Lodge, old log structures here are relatively few. They contribute significantly to the Southwest's architectural heritage. Like similarly-rare stone buildings, their comfort, native charm and scarcity make them especially worthy of preservation.

Hopi House, at the Grand Canyon (1905) Designed by Mary Colter, this may be the earliest modern building to consciously mimic the ancient architectural manner of the Indian Pueblos. Stone is not customarily used in Pueblo Revival, though it is in the nearby Hopi towns. (Special Collections, University of Arizona Library)

CHAPTER 7

REVIVAL STYLES

In the years following the turn of the century up to the present day, the revival of regional styles has had a strong impact on the face of Southwestern architecture. European-inspired revivalism has been largely the story of other American architecture throughout the 19th century, but only after the arrival of the railroad did the 'revivalist' impulse deliver its eclectic cornucopia to the West.

After a brief spate with the many faces of Victorian influence, the Southwest was probably the first area in the United States to generate the revival of its *own* indigenous styles (other than maybe New England, where traditional regional styles, such as the Saltbox have a continuous lineage from earliest examples up to the present day — and indeed, can be seen, by now, virtually everywhere else in the country as well).

The sources for the Southwest Revival styles were principally Pueblo-Spanish, Spanish Mission and Territorial. Both Pueblo-Spanish and Territorial have continued in popular use to this day, and a few of the buildings discussed in this chapter are not technically 'historic' (more than 50 years old). Whether some of the more flimsy recent buildings in Revival styles contribute to, or compromise an appreciation of the true historic artifact is an interesting question. But they are certainly visible on the built scene.

PUEBLO REVIVAL

The traditions of Pueblo and Spanish styles of construction continue well into the 20th century, and essentially, are still in practice today where 'folk,' do-it-yourself architecture survives. But in the early part of this century, a concurrent Pueblo Revival style was born. It became widely popularized, curiously, particularly among the non-indigenous Anglo cultural element, seeking something in demonstratively 'regional' taste. Whether a building of the 20th century is traditional Pueblo or Spanish, or whether it is Pueblo Revival, probably depends upon the point of view and cultural background of who is doing the building, and to a degree, on the complexity, ammenity and 'modernness' of the plan.

To set things straight here, the style is also called the Santa Fe Style (to which it is not exclusive), and the Pueblo-Spanish or Spanish-Pueblo Revival (which seems a bit complicated). As there is no non-Spanish-influenced Pueblo Indian architecture today anyway, and *pueblo* is a Spanish word referring to town — whether it be Indian or Hispanic — the label 'Pueblo Revival' seems reasonable, not to mention concise.

The first building widely accepted as Pueblo Revival was the 1908 remodel of Hodgin Hall at the University of New Mexico, an 1890 academic building in the style of Richardsonian Romanesque. More accurately, the Estufa was constructed on the same campus in 1906 (a Phi Beta Kappa secret society hall derived directly from the secret society religious houses of the Rio Grande Indian pueblos — the kiva), and two other puebloid buildings were erected at the University around 1906 and 1907.

Again earlier, 1905 saw the construction of Mary Colter's 'Hopi House' at the Grand Canyon in northern Arizona — quite explicitly based upon the existing stone construction of ancient Oraibi, in Hopi land. With Hopi nearby, and an Indian museum/showroom as

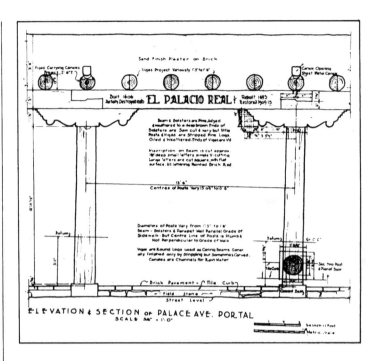

Detail of the Palace of the Governor's portal, as it was remodelled between 1911 and 1913. Earliest documentation seems to suggest that the original building had no portal at all. It is not known when the first one was built, but 19th century photographs show a progression from simple Territorial style through a multitude of Victorian embellishments.

By the early 20th century, movers in the newly-formed Museum of New Mexico decided it should be more regionally 'historical', and this portal is the result. Doors and windows remain Territorial. (Historic American Buildings Survey)

East half of the south elevation, Palace of the Governors (Historic American Buildings Survey)

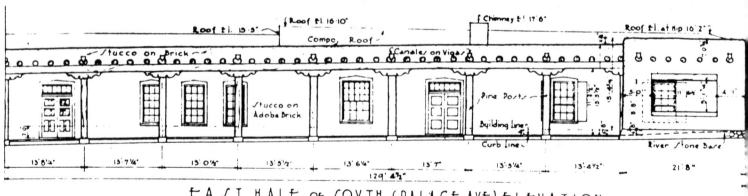

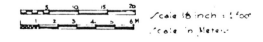

its function, she thought it would be appropriate to the site and program. About the same time, Rapp and Rapp designed a Pueblo Revival warehouse in Morley, Colorado; it was later re-interpreted into the New Mexico Building for the 1915 Panama California Exposition in San Diego. Designed along the lines of a 17th century mission church in the Indian pueblos, this basic design concept reached its fruition with the 1917 Museum of Fine Arts in Santa Fe, again by Rapp and Rapp.

Six years earlier, the Territorial/Victorian portal of the Palace of the Governors had been removed for a hypothetical reconstruction of its historic Spanish Colonial appearance (albeit romanticized and highly conjectural) by Museum Director Jesse Nusbaum and Sylvanus Morley, both influential advocates of architectural regionalism. Other fine institutional and commercial buildings of the Pueblo Revival include the La Fonda (1920), the Laboratory of Anthropology (1931), the New Mexico School for the Deaf (1935), and the National Park Service Headquarters (1939) all in Santa Fe; the Sagebrush Inn at Taos (1927); the WPA-period White Sands Visitor Center (1938), and the original Albuquerque airport terminal building (1939).

The De La Pena house in Santa Fe, built before 1845 (above). (Museum of New Mexico Photo Archives.)

The De La Pena house in 1980 (below). Around 1917, Frank Applegate began a renovation and expansion of the house, including a second floor. The second story veranda employed a replica of the existing first floor.

La Fonda, a sumptuous regional-style hotel in Santa Fe (1920), as it originally appeared.

The style became popular for residential construction from the 1920s on, particularly in Santa Fe and Albuquerque. A few examples — usually not as good — are seen as far west as Phoenix and Los Angeles, north to Denver, and an excellent one in Lubbock, Texas: the home of Dr. Curry Holden, appropriately, a Southwestern archaeologist. Among the most noteworthy, in Santa Fe, are the Carlos Vierra house, which received 2nd Place in a 1917 competition for a house in the (then still undefined) 'Santa Fe Style,' and the Emilia Hollenback house of 1930, designed by John Gaw Meem. It incorporated actual architectural elements salvaged from at least eight major 18th through 19th century structures reportedly, at least, in ruin at the time.

The keynote features of this new/old style were clustered, irregular massing, flat roofs, and setback of successive stories. A heavy, massive effect — with softly rounded corners, and thick battered (sloping) walls and parapets — was *de regle:* all intended to look like adobe, even if it weren't. Exposed wood lintels over doors and windows (never arches except in garden walls), buttresses, limited and controlled punctuation of the monolithic wall surfaces, projecting roof beams, and portales with round log columns and carved capitals, are all characteristic.

An array of other distinctive details fill it out, with elements borrowed from church architecture and elsewhere: corner towers, espanadas (cupolas for the church bell), carved wooden grills, chimney pots and even Pueblo-

Vierra house, showing the west portal: an effective way of reducing summer afternoon heat gain and creating a sunset-viewing space. The original mud plaster has been replaced — as frequently elsewhere — with cement stucco (Museum of New Mexico Photo Archives)

The Carlos Vierra house, on the Old Pecos Trail in Santa Fe (1917), a benchmark in domestic architecture of the Pueblo Revival. A large expanse of second-story windows (partially hidden by the parapet to the left) provide perfect north light for a two-story studio, but pose a drastic heat loss problem — suggesting the aesthetic priorities of the times, and the ability to overcome such follies with mechanical means, and plenty of energy.

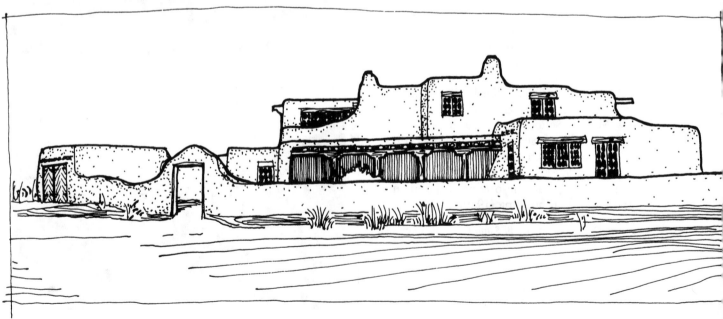

Exterior wood grill and dowelled ladder from the Sagebrush Inn at Taos: two of the finishing details requisite in successful rendition of the Pueblo Revival. This kind of picturesque, hand-crafted detail demands a high price tag today, unless of course, you do it all yourself.

Metal-studded wood door with iron grill, from the Sagebrush Inn. Though iron appears more frequently in the Pueblo Revival, it was very seldom used in buildings preceding the 1850s. It is more characteristic of Mexican architecture.

Interior ceiling from the White Sands National Monument Headquarters, a fine WPA-period building (1936-38). Though this particular type of three-tier treatment is uncommon, interiors of the period often have an elegance of detail unparalleled in more recent construction.

style ladders. Occasionally, Art Deco inflections appear in the geometricized rendition of rug and pottery designs for stained or polychromed wood carving, a variety of fixtures, tilework (as in the McKinley County Courthouse in Gallup) and furnishings (as in the superb original hotel carpets of the La Fonda in Santa Fe). Springing perhaps in part from the sensibilities of the American Craftsman movement, this regionalized version could achieve a richness beyond compare.

The overall intention was to create a visual effect rather like ancient Taos Pueblo, but with a lot more ammenity. Above all, it had to be plastered on the outside to look like adobe, though many period buildings are actually of fired brick or hollow clay tile. Later concrete block, wood frame, and later still, even steel framing with an applied veneer has been used, as in the Inn at Loretto Hotel in Santa Fe (1975-76).

Though the Pueblo Revival style remains popular today, particularly in luxury residences, the cost of materials and labor to produce these neo-primitive effects convincingly is usually prohibitive. Most of the best, most sensuous and enduring examples, were built between WWI and WWII. From the 1970s to the present day, another more simplified, popular offshoot has appeared: 'passive solar adobe,' which is discussed in the following Modern Regionalism.

MISSION REVIVAL

Spaniards built mission churches in the Indian pueblos in what are now the states of New Mexico and Arizona, from the early 1600s on. About 150 years later, they began the serious colonialization of other areas of the Southwest. By then, architectural fashion had changed, even in the remote provinces of future Texas, southern Arizona and California. The favor was for a more Baroque treatment than seen in earlier Colonial architecture, with arches, vaults, domes and heavily encrusted detailing — all in all, more in the character of Spanish construction in Mexico, to the south. This Spanish Colonial Baroque style was the first to be set upon as a source for the regional revivals of the 20th century.

Initiated in the mid-1890s in California, Mission Revival was soon adopted by the Santa Fe Railway Systems as the signature style of its station buildings. It spread from there. Note that the railroad, which brought the rage of imported styles in the last two decades of the 1800s, would, by 1900, identify the importance of perpetuating regionally relevant, not to mention romantic and commercially alluring architecture. This reversed, or at least tempered, the non-indigenous (actually, antinative) character of period construction.

One of the earliest and best examples of Mission Revival in the Southwest, the Alvarado Hotel, opened as the provincially posh Albuquerque Harvey House in 1902. It was demolished in 1970. (One of the sad chapters in urban renewal; one cannot help but think if it had survived today, the marvelous apprecia-

The Alvarado Hotel, In Albuquerque, under demolition in 1970. (Gordon Ferguson, Museum of New Mexico Photo Archives)

The Raton train station in eastern New Mexico, featuring the salient elements of the Mission Revival style: smooth plastered walls, arched colonnade, tower and the hallmark frontal gable with curved flourishes.

tion it might have enjoyed.) The Alvarado was designed by Charles Whittlesey (Whittlesey's own house is described in chapter 6). An adjacent Indian Building was decorated by Mary Colter, in the 'tastefully cluttered' manner suggestive of a 19th century frontier trading post — trend setting in its time for its explicit regionalism, proudly stated.

Other noteworthy examples of Mission Revival elsewhere in New Mexico are the Val Verde Hotel in Socorro (1919); the Castaneda in Las Vegas (1892); the Bronson Cutting House in Santa Fe (1911); and the Albuquerque, Raton, and some of the other major Santa Fe Railway Systems. Certain residential neighborhoods (12th Street NW in Albuquerque is a good example) sport a fanciful array of frontal Mission Revival gables — typical of the style — on otherwise anonymous bungalows, achieving in ensemble all the distinction due individual, important buildings.

Typical features of the style include large flat walls with isolated, complex detail, arches, towers and symmetrically curvilinear gables as monumental frontispieces. Exterior walls are often painted white or a bright pastel color, unlike the earth, or earth-tones of the Spanish—Pueblo and Territorial Revivals. Tile often appears as detail, or for complete roofs. Other off-shoots of the style include the Mediterranean (where large tile roofs supersede the visual dominance of the gables) and the post-1915 San Diego Panama California Exposition rendition of Spanish Baroque (as seen in the Lensic Theater in Santa Fe and, adapted with Indian and Art Deco motifs, the Kimo Theater in Albuquerque). Cushy shopping centers and commercial developments in Texas, and elsewhere throughout the Southwest, also bear the San Diego signature.

Other than the Mediterranean, which still has some popularity for domestic con-

Church in Lumberton, northern New Mexico. Dressed up rural folk-vernacular, with Mission overtones.

The Bronson Cutting house, Santa Fe, 1911. The solarium (behind the arches, at center) was once an open porch, capitalizing on both views and winter sun. (Museum of New Mexico Photo Archives)

Park Plaza Motel, Raton. Commercial vernacular in which monumental frontality — including splayed end 'pavillions' on the almost-endless facade — assumes movie set two-dimensionality: an arresting feature for which Mission Revival has a great propensity.

84

struction, the Mission Revival and related styles have generally lost favor since the 1950s. They seem to have taken on some of the stigma of kitsch; but like American cars with huge tail-fins of the 50s, Mission Revival designs may some day be accorded the respct of low High Art.

TERRITORIAL REVIVAL

The third of the major regional Revival styles is Territorial. Even more than the other two, it seems barely a revival, as the application of Greek Revival trim to indigenous buildings has, in remote areas at least, never ceased in popularity since its first introduction in the mid 1800s.

Territorial Revival buildings are essentially like the earlier, true period construction in appearance. On the adobe-colored surface (seldom are these structures actually of adobe) white trim detail — in pedimented doors and windows and colonnaded portal — reveals the spirit of Neoclassicism. Very simple. Perhaps the relatively easy application of these hallmark details to conventional contemporary building materials, particulary cement block and wood frame accounts for its current popularity, especially in commercial and institutional structures. The sensuous lines and rusticated handcraftmanship of Pueblo Revival are not as well suited to the flatness and angularity of industrialized materials and are far more costly to include as cosmetics. Also, the box-like form and regularity of window treatment in the Territorial seems better adapted to the modern economy of enclosing more space with fewer, and more standardized materials. Hence, its popularity for schools,

government buildings, and larger commercial structures. Despite its graceful style and economic rationale, Territorial Revival is almost exclusive to New Mexico, seldom appearing elsewhere in the Southwest.

The major difference, aside from construction technology, between 19th and 20th century Territorial lies primarily in scale and detail. Period Territorial buildings are never large by contemporary standards; but today's buildings are so substantially larger that even other shapes have emerged, such as the massive donut of the New Mexico State Capitol building. Likewise, detail is rendered on a much larger scale, sometimes poorly, and sometimes with a much greater academic correctness than during the Territorial period. Even the foliated capitals of Corinthian come

Monumental doorway in Corinthian style, from the old St. Vincent Hospital in Santa Fe. Most of the rest of the building is rendered with more banal rationality. (The door — one of the few elegant features in the design — is seen as insensitively filled-in during a 1983 renovation.)

into play, and a few buildings assume almost Baroque complexity in their allusion to the Neoclassic.

Of the more straightforward, classically Territorial designs of the Revival era, the Berardinelli Building in Santa Fe must be counted among the best. Built in 1936, and designed by accomplished regionalist architect John Gaw Meem, the building achieves an astonishing unity within a complex and diverse program. Municipal offices, courtrooms, a police headquarters and jail, and even a fire station, are housed within a single handsomely-scaled, two-story block with projecting side wings (a classic Palladian device frequently employed by Meem).

A two-story colonnade gracefully highlights the main western elevation, set back from the street and flanked by the lower extending wings. Detailing throughout (the exterior at least, for the interior has been drastically remodelled — sadly, a tribute to the inherent adaptability of the basic design) is

The Berardinelli Building by John Gaw Meem (1936). Territorial Revival appeared on the scene later than Pueblo or Mission Revivals. In this structure for the City of Santa Fe, Meem achieved both a sensible and elegant plan solution and a consummate expression of Territorial style brought into the 20th century. Its historicism is more literal than most later examples of the style, and is achieved with simpler means.

excellent. No matter what style in which it was rendered — for it could have been any of many (imagine it for example, as Romanesque or a streamlined Moderne building, as seen in California, with 'porthole' windows and so forth) — Meem's Berardinelli Building seems like a very good piece of architecture.

Though John Gaw Meem was a master of Pueblo Revival — usually sparing many of the cute-isms which characterize that style, with a preference for good, clear massing and discrete detail — many of his later institutional and larger residential projects are in the manner of Territorial Revival. As mentioned, one of his favorite *partis* (or generalized building

configurations) was the Italian Renaissance Palladian central block with flanking symmetrical wings: well-suited to the Neoclassicism of Territorial, though seldom, if ever, used in period buildings of the 19th century.

One of the flanking wings could as easily be a fire station — as represented in the Berardinelli Building — or a household garage — as seen in the Stewart Harvey house in Santa Fe, where a New England style doorcase, with broken pediment and center pedistal with urn, lavishes atypical (Georgian) finesse to the main entrance. A similar, centralized scheme was employed by Meem for Las Poblanos, the palatial western home of the Simms-McCormick family in Albuquerque's north valley. Like the luscious warmth of early Pueblo Revival, it seems that few buildings of the late 20th century compare well to the cool elegance of the Southwest's Territorial style, as revisited in the 30s and 40s.

The New Mexico Supreme Court: identifiable Neo-classic detail at the entry, with some surprises on the interior.

Library elevation of the New Mexico Supreme Court. Typical of most Territorial Revival, modern industrial design elements are also incorporated; in this case, black glass panels hide the intermediate floors, enhancing the impression of long continuous pillasters on the facade.

Detail of center-folding windows on the New Mexico Supreme Court Building.

Plan schematic of the Val Verde Hotel, one of the relatively few Revival Style buildings with some apparent solar design characteristics.

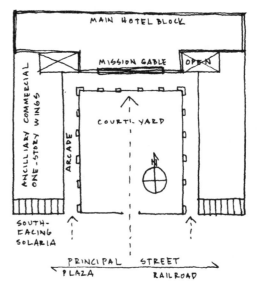

One of the oldest inhabited solar houses in America, dating from the 1950s. Designed by Peter van Dresser — certainly one of the most innovative thinkers in regionally appropriate technology — an old (north-south axis) adobe house was retrofitted with integrated rooftop collectors.

ENERGY & THE REVIVAL STYLES

Buildings of the Revival styles are seldom any more impressive in terms of intrinsic energy efficiency than their historic antecedents: often less so. Of course, if they are actually built of adobe, they have the thermal-mass characteristic which has perpetuated fondness for earth construction in spite of its disadvantages. But more often, Revival style buildings are of lighter weight materials — representing a generation of more 'advanced' building practice.

For example, the modern petroleum-based built-up roof is superior to the traditional earth roof for insulation and keeping water out, but without the mass, less effective for thermal storage. Generally speaking, orientation drifts away from a southerly pattern. Occasionally, some vague preference is given to south-facing glass, but architectural decisions are more often predicated on aesthetic tenets: views are more likely to determine massing than prevailing winds or solar exposure.

Among the seemingly notable exceptions is the Val Verde Hotel in Socorro, New Mexico. Situated on the north side of the major east-west street running between the plaza and the railroad, the exposure is good for solar gain, though seldom is it elsewhere optimized in period commercial buildings. In the Val Verde, a rather modern, if somewhat banal, exposed cement brick is used to surface the slightly diluted Mission Revival building (similar to the candor with which Bernard Maybeck used industrial materials to finish essentially Romantic buildings in California a few decades earlier). The overall layout of the plan is nice, with loggias surrounding an entrance garden, and it all seems direct and sincere, if perhaps plain.

What lends distinction to the Val Verde in terms of solar design is the detailing of the south walls of the extending wings, forming the courtyard: within the technical limitations of the times, the walls and a small part of the roof are virtually all glass. Only these areas — representing a relatively small percentage of the overall building surface — are executed in this manner suggesting architectural intention. Even for street-front commercial space, the deliberate creation of 'solarium' rooms is quite uncommon — particularly in the Mission style, where solid wall surface is generally punctuated by relatively small window areas. The commercial spaces behind these glass walls are wonderful.

In terms of cooling and natural ventilation, we might look to the New Mexico Supreme Court Building in Santa Fe for a good example. Built in 1936-37 in the Territorial Revival style, and attributed to architect Gordon Street, the design is rather clever in layout and planning — of the major spaces at least — and its use of 'modernized' Greek detail. Though certain signature features of the Territorial appear, the buildig is quite unlike anything emerging from the early U.S. occupation of the southwest. Giant, splayed wings frame the diagonal entrance, which has some fairly representative Territorial detailing. From there, the design is primarily 1930s Moderne with regional overtones, mostly in richly executed decorative embellishments.

The most interesting space is the impressive three-story law library, with tiered balconies, on axis with the main entrance. Here, the high volume of the central void is vented by clerestory windows at the top, creating a constant draft of fresh air through the balcony alcoves below, for summer ventilation. Windows are cleverly conceived to fold toward the center, creating a virtual 100% aperture. (Natural cooling doesn't work very well these days, one hears, probably because the source of fresh air is directly off a large, unshaded parking area.) The south elevation of this wing features large areas of glass. Interestingly, in order to achieve a sense of massive continuous pilasters on the facade, the structural spandrel areas between the floors are clad on the exterior in black glass (four-lites, like the windows themselves) — almost 15 years before Skidmore, Owings & Merrill established the treatment as a modern classic on buildings in New York and Chicago.

In general, it seems that buildings of the 1900-1940 Revival period tend to indulge themselves in the 'cheap energy' philosophy of the times. Not until the 1970s would the Pueblo Revival, in particular, re-emerge as a popular acceptable image for a further energy-conscious renewal. As of the early 1980s, among the three major Southwestern Revival styles, only the Mission Revivial has lost its popularity. It is doubtless due for another breath of life: the Post-Modern fascination

with facades — for which Mission is the unassailable king in the Southwest — seems to assure that its rediscovery is near at hand. A Mission Revival revival.

MODERN REGIONALISM

The 20th century Revival styles form an important bridging generation between the historic and modern. The potentials of a regional modernism were already evident by the 1930s, in such examples as the Wheelwright Museum in Santa Fe (then the award-winning Museum of Navajo Ceremonial Art) — a giant, abstracted Navajo hogan — and the McKinley County Courthouse in Gallup, with its almost Post-Modern Mannerist detached facade. The fusion of historic regionalism with

Adobe house by the team of David Wright and Karen Terry: semi-subterranean and puebloid.

modern architecture continues to this day, and appears to be finding its most established expression in the 'solar adobe' idiom.

A recent generation of high-mass passive solar buildings — primarily derivative of the Pueblo Revival, but incorporating large areas of south-facing glass — suggests an adapted, and perhaps new, regional style. Blending indigenous elements, materials and details with intermediate passive solar technology, these are the most thermally efficient buildings to date in the Southwest. (The phrase 'most energy-efficient' would be inaccurate in comparison to, say, 18th century Indian Pueblo architecture; transportation to suburban sites, appliances, lighting, trips to the grocery store, garage door openers, et al., contribute to an overall energy profile which is hundreds-fold more consumptive than the traditional Pueblo house unit, despite the 'efficiency' of the building itself.)

Another house by Wright-Terry, in which the passive solar-adobe idiom exhibits some finesse in the blending of old and new.

Just the same, what we see in the passive solar wing of modern regionalism is a truly sincere architecture which transcends the fundamentally Romantic imagery of earlier revivals: striving to achieve a reasoned insight into the use of technology, materials and form.

SUMMARY:
CONCLUDING THE HISTORIC FILE

This chapter has briefly surveyed almost 1000 years of architectural history in the American Southwest — with an emphasis on the representative particulars of New Mexico — both in terms of architectural style and simple forms of energy technology. Style reflects what people are thinking about: social values and aspirations, concepts of man in relationship with nature, and ideas about our own past. Various applications of energy technology — however simple by today's standards — tell us something about how clever a particular population was, where its resource priorities lay, and how much people thought they could afford to waste.

Certainly, vast strides have been made in the comfort level of all buildings. Many new ideas in design have come into play, most at a cost of increased, non-renewable, energy consumption. Where solid conceptual building blocks already existed, often they were cast aside for the new. Consider, for example, the 1000-year-old Anasazi town type: attached townhouses, terraced to the south — an idea which is being resurrected today — and often being considered original in high-density urban designs. Or the single-file Spanish Colonial house, east-west on axis, as seen in the Penasco Valley, which was abandoned among its own originators as soon as the railroad provided the materials for longer roof spans, and non-orientation specific plans.

Post-modern architecture all over the world is reaching into the regional and historic archives to restore life, imagery and human content to its buildings. The Southwest may take some pride in having been among the first in the Modern epoch to appreciate the vir-

tues of its own native traditions. But in this flirtation with the past, it is important to look beyond the appearance of things — to the fundamental rationale of *why* things were done. With folk-building forming the backbone of the Southwest's architectural heritage, design rationale is often very close to the surface. On the frontier, life was marginal: waste was not only in bad taste, it was impractical. The frontier has closed in, and we are once again reminded of a world of limited resources. The past holds many lessons, if only we are wise enough to learn them.

Now, how to take care of the Southwest's old buildings: rare, instructive and irreplaceable physical and cultural resources. Part II of this book addresses preservation of historic buildings, particularly those adobe.

Part III follows with an analysis of remodeling and solar retrofitting — a realistic strategy, and properly done, not necessarily at odds with the integrity of the Southwest's historic structures.

The La Luz housing compound, on the west mesa of Albuquerque (1968-74). Designed by Antoine Predock, almost every aspect of this compound is masterful in its modern interpretation of adobe construction, from phased site plan to exposed-aggregate concrete bond beams.

PART II:
HISTORIC PRESERVATION IN THE SOUTHWEST: A HANDS-ON HANDBOOK

INTRODUCTION:
MAINTAINING & REVIVING THE OLD ADOBE BUILDING

With a growing interest in historic preservation in America, a number of good sources of information have emerged to assist the homeowner, builder and construction professional. Some of these are listed in the bibliography. Few of the books and other publications, however, contain material specific to the Southwest's very distinctive building heritage — adobe construction in particular — and much of what exists is not easily obtainable (being somewhat obscure government reports, and so forth.)

The following chapters attempt to illuminate a long legacy of unwritten folk-tradition, published and unpublished information on managing the preservation and restoration of old buildings in the Southwest. Preservation techniques common to buildings everywhere — such as those appropriate to doors and windows — are treated briefly, with reference to the specifics of regional traditions. Given more in-depth discussion are concerns unique to buildings in this area — particularly those of adobe. Earth walls and flat roofs contribute immeasurably to the architectural character of the region. At the same time, they are a genuine challenge to maintain.

The presence today of earth buildings which are hundreds of years old seems to clearly demonstrate that traditional maintenance and preservation techniques work. But new materials and preservation technologies have appeared and are in use, frequently comingled with the old ways. Sometimes they are effective for historic structures, and sometimes not. The treatment of ancient earth walls with silicon may be of questionable integrity, and seems extremely odd at least. At the same time, occasionally these newfangled approaches are the only viable options.

Traditional approaches to preservation and maintenance of historic structures are almost always a sure bet; and while they may be bothersome, done in the do-it-yourself pattern of former days, with local materials, they are usually cheap. They never seem to become outdated. Mud plaster is still a great way to finish an adobe wall.

Despite the flamboyant excesses of Stephen Dorsey (see Chapter 4) and a few other people who did not seem to comprehend where they were, American propensities for waste and overconsumption have never been considered particularly tasteful in the Southwest — even among those who could afford it. The frontier ethic of frugality, popular by necessity if not cultural tradition, still lives today, though a once-characteristic understatement now often assumes, shall we say, a much higher profile in glamourized 'ethnicity.'

In the following chapters, a fair amount of consideration is paid to the issue of energy and conservation, for this is one of the principal reasons people today mess with old buildings to begin with. Loose-fitting doors waste energy, as do heated but unused rooms. But this needn't mean that one go out and buy a $60 solid core door at a builders' supply store — and throw away the historic artifact — in order to effect a tight building. Ideas on resolving the occasional conflict between historic preservation *and* energy conservation are suggested here, but a great deal depends upon the attitudes and living habits of the occupants.

Chapters in this *How-To* section are laid out with an historic overview of the specific building elements being discussed, followed by a series of typical problems and solution strategies. Though it is hoped that for many situations this will be an adequate do-it-yourself handbook, some conditions call for professional assistance — from a designer, architect or engineer — and this is usually well worth the investment.

An assessment of a particular building's artistic or historic worth may seem somewhat subjective. But to everyone, his own building is a unique resource. And importantly, the older, rarer or historically significant a structure, the more it deserves careful attention in any preservation, rehabilitation, addition or adaptive use. Aside from the fortunate survival of historic *styles* to the present day, the real thing — the old building — is an irreplaceable treasure.

The adobe walls of a Spanish frontier hacienda.

CHAPTER 8

WALLS

Traditions of native wall construction in the Southwest include earth, stone, and wood as materials. Pre-Columbian Indians built of all three, with localized cultural preferences and available resources customarily determining the nature of preferred materials. Where good building rock was available, structures were usually built of stone, often with mud chinking. Likewise, where proper adobe soils and sufficient water were abundant — such as in the Indian pueblos of the Rio Grande Valley — adobe was customarily used. Higher elevations, with more substantial stands of straight timber, in the following Spanish and Anglo periods, usually suggest a higher frequency of log construction. Among these materials, adobe is in most widespread use today.

This chapter concentrates on the preservation and conservation issues of adobe walls, as these form the fundamental and most problematic portion of the historic regional architecture. Stone and log construction involve their own preservation technologies, and these are covered more extensively elsewhere (See Bibliography.) Just the same, problems such as deterioration due to water — perhaps the principal enemy of most building materials — and appropriate solutions — such as drainage, may find these pages helpful.

THE ADOBE WALL

Just prior to colonization by the Spaniards in the 16th and 17th centuries, many Pueblo Indian walls were made of essentially the same adobe material as used today — but they were 'puddled' — laid up in successive hand-packed courses (similar to *pise*; rammed earth — but without the containing forms which are

93

raised with the courses). A few of these structures survive, mostly in ruin, including the massive Casa Grande in Arizona. Rammed earth (employing formwork) enjoyed a very modest popularity in the 1920s and 30s, and the rare surviving examples of this technology seem especially worthy of preservation.

Spanish colonial settlement, and establishment of missions in the Indian pueblos, introduced the technique of forming the Puebloans' traditional adobe mud into separate bricks, 'baked' in the sun. While material composition was identical to the puddled antecedent, the mass-produced modular brick made construction faster and, in many ways more convenient. Also, corners at adjacent walls were now bonded together (rather than built separately, as had been done previously), making for sturdier structures. Brick sizes vary somewhat by locality and historical period, but they were always large enough to expedite construction and small enough to be handled by one man, without breaking. (Size and composition may be a general indication of the age of a building — though bricks were often recycled, and will therefore appear in structures dating later than the original brick manufacture.)

Along the Rio Grande, and more rarely in other areas of the Southwest, another form of earth construction was also practiced. Around Albuquerque and to the south, especially Isleta Pueblo, *terrones* — mud and sod blocks cut from grassy river bottoms (not unlike the 'soddies' of the 19th century frontier Great Plains) — were used. Though *terron*, or 'turtle-back,' construction is still practiced at Isleta, later examples of the technology are relatively scarce elsewhere (the Yott and Allen houses in Albuquerque are good examples of the technique as practiced by Anglos) and deserve special attention in preservation.

Adobe is composed of three elements: *caliche* or clay, as a bonding agent; sand or fine gravel for compressive strength; and straw, horsehair, grasses, pine needles, or other organic fiber, primarily as an agent to prevent cracking during curing. The proportions vary

The traditional adobe-making process. After sifting, materials are mixed to the correct proportions. Next it is poured wet into forms. Hand packing fills the cells uniformly. While still wet, the forms are removed. Adobe bricks are set on edge, and rotated for drying. Finished bricks are stacked to cure and await construction.

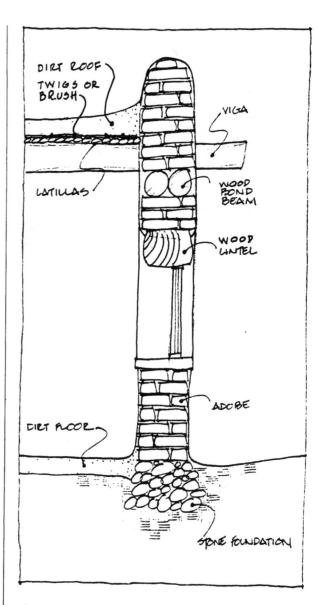

— and the plant fiber may be left out entirely — but generally they are about 20-30% clay, 50-60% sand or fine gravel, 3% straw or fiber, and 17% water. The water evaporates out as the brick and wall dry.

Historically, adobe walls were constructed in the following manner: a footing of round or flat stone is laid in a shallow trench, to inhibit the capillary action of ground water, rising up from the earth around the base of the wall. These footings may extend to below frost line (as is common in contemporary building practice), but this is seldom the case in older historic buildings. Sometimes adobe walls were laid with no footing at all; but naturally, few of these expediently conceived buildings are still standing today. If an old building is still existing and in sound structural shape, it probably has an adequate foundation. Just the same, due to the destructive effects of water on adobe, shallow footings are often one of the most problematic areas; change in the water table due to natural or man-made causes can undermine even stable old walls.

Above stone footings, adobe bricks are laid, usually in running bond, with a similar mud used as mortar. When walls cure, they form a more or less monolithic mass — provided the materials are essentially the same in composition. As adobe bonds to little but itself, any dissimilarity in mortar and brick composition — as in the use of Portland cement mortar by ill-advised latter day builders — eventually traps water and caues deterioration of the load-bearing adobe. Trouble, as we shall see.

Adobe wall thickness varies from ten inches to three feet or more. Many older buildings have rather thick walls, employing two or more bricks in depth, occasionally with an insulating air, or rubble-filled cavity. Higher earth walls are of necessity thicker. Buttresses are occasionally used where cross walls are absent for lateral support, along high walls, or at critical stress points, such as corners or large openings.

Adobe walls are good in compressive strength but worthless in tensile strength. (In other words — unlike wood or steel — they can't even support their own weight when hung from the top.) In order to distribute point loads of roof beams or rafters more evenly

through the bearing wall, a horizontal wooden beam. Chunks of adobe bricks are fitted between peeled-log *vigas* or squared roof beams; and on flat-roofed buildings, an adobe or brick parapet continues up to finish the wall. Where tween peeled-log *vigas* or squared roof beams; and on flat-roofed buildings, an adobe or brick parapet continues up to finish the wall. Where openings occur at doors and windows, a timber lintel is usually found; frequently in later periods, complete with rough jambs, tied into the walls with 'gringo blocks' (chunks of wood inserted in place of adobe to provide an anchor for nailing). Adobe arches and vaults are found in some areas of the Spanish Southwest — Arizona, Texas, and California in particular; but they never gained any wide popularity in New Mexico, except in Mission Revival buildings, most of which are not built with adobe.

95

PLASTERS & STUCCOS

In historic tradition, walls were finished with a coat — or perhaps several coats — of mud or lime plaster. If given occasional renewal, mud or lime plaster is probably still the best known technique for preserving the structural adobe; indeed, it becomes *part* of the structural wall. With these finishes, when there are problems they become immediately apparent: maybe unsightly but diagnostically valuable. Additionally, the weathered appearance of mud plaster lends a naturalistic, earth-integrated sincerity that later cement stucco finishes cannot hope to replicate.

Pale clays were ususally mixed with lime or gypsum for interior plaster, in both Indian and Spanish buildings. Smooth trowelled, the finish provided virtually white walls for maximum reflectance of what little light entered through the limited fenestration. Earth-colored dados were frequently painted on the lower part of the wall, or in the Spanish and later eras, fabric might be applied here to inhibit rubbing off of the chalky plaster in this area most susceptible to contact. Lime plaster was also used — occasionally with a similar dado — beneath portals for decorative enhancement. All of these treatments, dating back several hundred years, are still in practice where a regionalist enthusiasm exists.

With the 20th century Revival styles, cement stucco was introduced as a 'technical improvement' over traditional mud plaster, creating a hard surface which repelled water and did not require the same regular maintenance. Despite its advantages, the hard stucco introduced some new problems; primarily its failure to actually bond with the adobe masonry, and its propensity for trapping water inside the vulnerable earth wall.

With cement or hard plaster finishes, metal mesh or lath is nailed to the adobe wall (in a somewhat tenuous bond). Then at least two coats of stucco are applied, with the final coat tinted, usually an earth tone (or sometimes painted, for a less convincing effect). As concrete is less permeable to water, once moisture gets inside the hard finish, it can cause continuous structural deterioration, while the surface itself may look perfectly sound. It is essential to seal all cracks in a hard stucco immediately as they develop. Failure to do so hastens structural problems. This unfortunate — and often unseen — handicap causes many experts to consider cement inferior to mud for the preservation of adobe walls. Related problems and solutions with various finish coat materials are outlined in the following sections.

GENERAL OVERVIEW OF PROBLEMS WITH ADOBE WALLS

The principal problems with adobe walls are keeping water out, and keeping heat in. Problems with water, and its resultant structural damage, are covered in the following section on preservation; problems of heat loss are discussed in the section on conservation. Whatever the problem or appropriate solution, several things must be borne in mind. As with all work on historic structures, it is essential to research and document the building first, as suggested in the section Research and Documentation of Historic Buildings (Appendix A).

Cracks or other symptoms of problems which are stable — that is, not in a noticeably changing mode — may not be serious enough to demand drastic and immediately conceived solutions; observing changes in the building is essential. Do the areas adjacent to cracks seem to be moving over a period of weeks or years, or is it a basically stable condition? If the wall is cracked but stable, simple infill and patching may suffice; but if the condition appears to be changing, more serious structural problems will have to be addressed.

Water returns adobe to wet mud, so the most critical zones with earth walls are in areas where water is most likely to be present. The best preservation techniques address these problems: the maintenance of the protective coating, whether it is mud, plaster or or cement stucco; solid footings and appropriate drainage to inhibit capillary action; and a good roof.

Adobe walls are fundamentally a reshaped and slightly hardened version of the earth itself, and they tend to return to their original state. Conscientious maintenance is a requisite in all preservation. Beyond routine maintenance, any preservation effort should embody a comprehensive understanding of all related problems, as attention to one area and not another may actually magnify deterioration.

Adobe does not bond with much other than itself, and modestly at that. All materials used in conjunction with adobe walls — including the traditional wood and stone — are essentially incompatible in bonding, and it is at the juncture of materials that deterioration will most likely occur. Addition of incompatible materials — such as replacing missing or deteriorated adobe wall sections with stablized adobe, concrete block, or Portland cement mortar — is likely to aggravate the situation, often advancing its demise. This might even include the addition of cement stucco, and perhaps insulation, but professional opinion and practice vary widely on this subject. The following section on conservation addresses hazards inherent in insulating adobe.

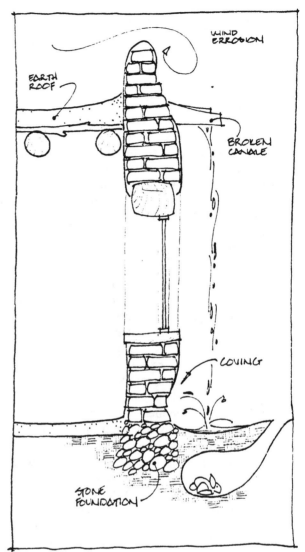

Composite view of typical adobe building deterioration, and its causes.

Problem 1:
Basic Deterioration & Maintenance of Plaster & Stucco

Erosion due to the environmental stresses of wind and water is inevitable in adobe buildings with mud plaster finishes, and basic maintenance is the best solution. Problems and solutions for hard cement stucco are different. Maintaining the integrity of this protective skin is the key to keeping water, with its resultant structural damage, away from the structural adobe.

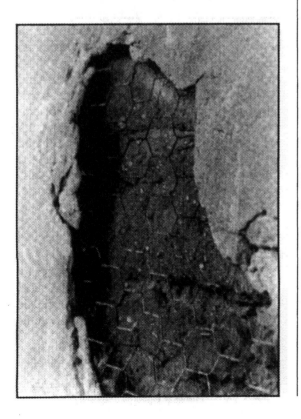

Cement stucco suggests more permanence than mud, but has its own problems: separation from the wall, trapping water beneath the finish, and disguising structural problems in the adobe itself.

Solution A:
Replastering A Mud Wall

Adobe plaster should be composed of materials similar to those of the wall itself. Colors may vary locally, and efforts should be made to use earth available nearby, if this would likely have been used in the original construction. Proportions should be: about 40% caliche; 60% sand, some pine needles or straw for a modest amount of tensile strength and even drying; and enough water to form a thick paste, capable of sticking to existing plaster or exposed adobe bricks. Mud surfaces to which plaster is applied are often lightly scored, and should be moistened to encourage an effective bond. Existing sections of plaster should be matched for composition, color, texture, and finished appearance.

Plaster is applied by hand or with a trowel; traditionally it is often 'polished' to a smooth surface with deer or sheepskins, and small slightly rounded stones. In seriously eroded areas, a scratch coat should be applied first, with a finish coat over. For a more detailed description of plastering technique, see references in the Bibliography. A good mud plaster will last from 2 to 15 years, depending upon the exposure, local weather, and the quality of the work.

Patching of especially worn areas, or entire single sides of a building, may also be done; these jobs should be done with care to best match existing materials. Areas most likely to require this treatment are the base and top of the wall, corners, around doors and windows, and sides of the building most exposed to prevailing winds and effects of erosion. If historic documentation indicates the presence of any form of coping at the top of a wall — either brick, stone, or perhaps tile — it should certainly be retained or restored, as it adds architectural character to the structure, and will retard the erosion of the wall surface.

Solution B:
Patching A Cement Stucco Wall

Small cracks in cement stucco will admit water into the wall, and the water-tightness of the stucco often traps it there. It is important to patch all cracks immediately, if only tem-

Obvious cracks in a mud wall can make the occupant very nervous. If minor or stable, they are easily repaired. If more drastic, sudden — or still expanding — more serious action is probably necessary.

98

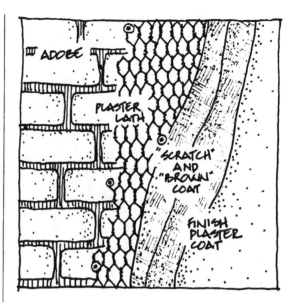

porarily. Cracks due to simple expansion and contraction are likely to occur at any of the typical stress points, including over or around doors and windows, at corners, on top of the parapet, or along the wall surface.

Large cracks probably indicate a serious structural condition underneath, and it may be necessary to remove the stucco around the affected area to make repairs there first. However, because cement stucco is not substantially bonded to the wall, a crack in the surface may indicate structural problems in another area of the wall, over which the stucco may appear perfectly sound. So while spot-patching may improve the cosmetic appearance of the building, and inhibit the further intrusion of water, it may do little in addressing the structural problems causing the cracking.

A typical condition may be a bulging crack at the base of the wall, indicating that the adobe beneath is probably giving way under load and moisture. The stucco must be removed and the adobe attended to first, as outlined in Problem 3, before the stucco is patched.

Stucco is usually applied in the following manner: nails are driven into the adobe wall, and expanded metal lath or chicken wire is attached. The plaster is laid onto the mesh in two or more coats; each coat is allowed to cure and then is moistened before applying the next. The scratch coat is left with a rough or raked surface to improve bonding with successive coats. Care should be taken in all patching to match existing finishes. Suppliers of materials will have more information on their application. This same method is also used in any stucco work done as smaller patches. Various bitumen tars are also used, as is a fiberglass reinforced cloth, over which the stucco is applied. Partcular attention should be paid to parapets and bases of walls, where cracking is common and water especially deterious.

Solution C:
Replacing Cement Stucco

Any moisture in the adobe wall will eventually cause the nails curing the metal mesh to rust away, releasing the nominal bond which exists, and causing extensive cracking and deformation of the cement stucco surface. Single sections, full walls, or entire buildings may eventually need to be resurfaced in the manner described in Solution B. If fairly sound, new work may be applied over old, but if structural problems are suggested by major cracking, the entire old plaster and mesh should be removed first.

Cement stucco can be deceptive in indicating the condition of the structure beneath. In the classic case of the famous Ranchos de Taos Church, an apparently good coat of cement plaster applied in 1966 (intended to reduce maintenance), hid serious deterioration

A concrete cap applied to this adobe parapet was intended to reduce erosion, but has simply changed its nature, including channeling a crack to the key stress points of the projecting viga.

99

of the adobe wall and buttress beneath. When it was finally discovered that inside the stucco was a vast hollowed cavity, the concern was that the entire wall might collapse — though it appeared sound on the surface. The solution was to remove the cement stucco and mesh entirely, and replaster with mud (which will immediately show any structural problems on the surface); restoring the building to its original form, using finishing techniques similar to those employed in its original construction. This may be considered as a good preservation method in any building with structural problems or a seriously deteriorated stucco finish.

Solution D:
Renewing or Restoring
Whitewash & Lime Plaster

In historic buildings of adobe or wood, whitewash and lime plasters have often been used as a finish, particularly on the interior of the walls. Their primary asset — aside from making interior spaces lighter than earthtone adobe plaster — is that they provide a harder coating to deter erosion, while still allowing the transpiration of water which might otherwise cause structural damage.

Lime plaster is applied by scoring the mud diagonally to about 1½'' (a hatchet makes a good tool), filling the crevices with lime mortar and stone or tile chips, and trowelling on a heavy coat of the plaster. The final coat may be applied in a thin slip (souplike consistency), or finished with stones and sheepskins, for a polished finish known as *alisado*. Whitewash is painted directly onto the mud brick or plaster.

A more water-resistent lime plaster is occasionally seen on historic buildings in higher and wetter locales. Though more durable than mud, no finish lasts forever unmaintained.

RECIPES:

Lime Plaster

Lime plaster is more durable than mud, and can be applied directly over adobe walls.

- *Slake 44 pounds of hydrated lime in 6 gallons of water for at least 24 hours. If any lumps remain, screen them out.*

- *Into one part of this lime paste, add 3 parts fine sand. Mix thoroughly, adding only enough water to form a workable, putty-like consistency. Apply to wall with trowel.*

Whitewash

- *Prepare 8 gallons of lime paste, by slaking 50 pounds of hydrated lime in 6 gallons of water overnight.*

- *Mix up 3 gallons of skim milk from a boxed powder.*

- *Into the skim milk, dissolve 3 pounds of TSP (trisodium phosphate, a heavy-duty cleaning compound, available at most builder's supply stores.)*

- *Stir the milk/TSP solution into the lime paste.*

- *Just before using, dissolve 3 pints of formaldehyde in 3 gallons of water. Very slowly add this solution to the other. Stir constantly and vigorously. Mix only enough for one day's painting at a time, for it doesn't keep.*

Problem 2:
Erosion at the Base of the Wall

Erosion at the base of adobe walls is common, due both to capillary action of ground water seeping up into the wall and because of the splash of water on the adjacent ground,

Coving at the base of an adobe wall.

100

causing coving. In the case of capillary action, which is common in buildings with poor foundations, water rises naturally in the wall; if water concentrations are above 20%, the structure can actually turn to mud, unable to support the weight above it.

Water in the wall can freeze and thaw in a daily cycle, and expanded crystalline ice will continuously flake off pieces of the wall. This is called *spalling*. Particularly if mud plaster has been used, water patches will be visible, and this is better than if hidden. If moisture content is believed to be high, some form of monitoring or measuring may be necessary to see just how serious this problem actually is.

Solution A:
Replace Adobe in Coved or Spalled Base of Wall

If damage appears modest and gradual, adobe plaster can, in many cases be renewed. Conventional wisdom might suggest the continual replacement of earth from the ground back onto the wall from which it fell, however the presence of salt and minerals distilled from groundwater will diminish its bonding capacity considerably. Therefore, if areas around the coved or spalled section show whitish powdery areas, eroded soil is probably too high in soluble minerals to use; new earth, of matching color, must be brought to the site for replastering.

In the case of serious coving, additional adobes may be fitted into the cove, carefully built as a structural wall, with the necessary footing. (Note: do not disturb existing footing or the earth it bears on.) Occasionally, this supplementary wall protrudes as a horizontal buttress. Make sure adobes, mortar, and plaster are compatible with existing materials.

Solution B:
Provide New Footings for Existing Walls

This is a realistic, though difficult solution; it may be necessary if there are signs of major structural cracking, or danger of wall collapse. CONSULT A SPECIALIST!

Three degrees of repair to a coved adobe wall. The third would benefit by some professional consultation. It can be dangerous!

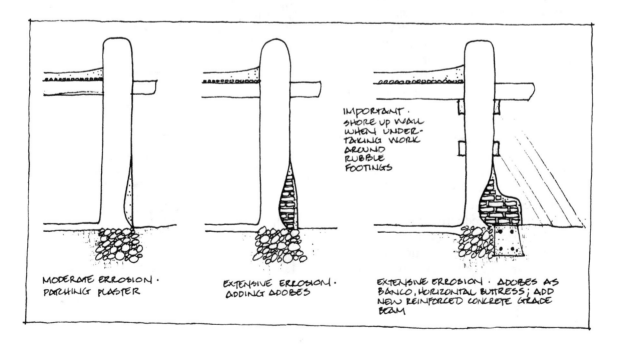

MODERATE ERROSION. PATCHING PLASTER

EXTENSIVE ERROSION. ADDING ADOBES

IMPORTANT. SHORE UP WALL WHEN UNDERTAKING WORK AROUND RUBBLE FOOTINGS

EXTENSIVE ERROSION. ADOBES AS BANCO, HORIZONTAL BUTTRESS; ADD NEW REINFORCED CONCRETE GRADE BEAM

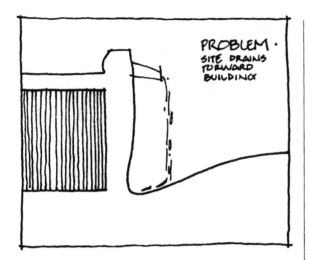

PROBLEM.
SITE DRAINS
TORWARD
BUILDING

The basic problem of poor site grading, and four solution strategies. In each case, the idea is to get water away from the vulnerable adobe walls. The retrieval or use of diverted water would be an additional benefit.

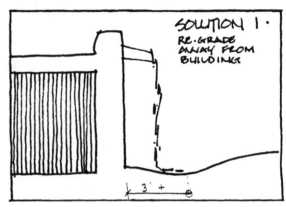

SOLUTION 1.
RE-GRADE
AWAY FROM
BUILDING

3'

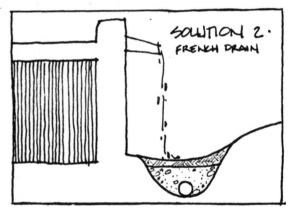

SOLUTION 2.
FRENCH DRAIN

Solution C:
Modify Drainage or Grading

Modifying drainage may be the simplest and most effective way of addressing inherent problems with groundwater. Obviously, water should run away from the building and not toward it. Some grading may be required, but one should avoid drastic alterations in the existing landscape which might adversely affect the building's particular historic character. A reasonable approach for drainage grading is suggested in the accompanying drawing.

A more complex — though more effective — solution would involve digging out a trench, and lining it with a French drain: tile or perforated pipe sloped to carry ground water away. The trench is filled with gravel, and sometimes covered with a layer of earth. This may be the most sensible way to protect footings without major modification of the structure itself. If well drained, even old walls with virtually no footings stand a much better chance of continued survival. Care must be taken not to disturb the earth on which the wall is bearing; follow the suggested section in this procedure.

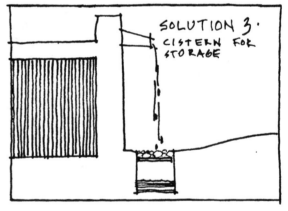

SOLUTION 3.
CISTERN FOR
STORAGE

One area of acute erosion is often at the base of the wall where canales drop the roof water. Splash stones, similar to those used historically in the Indian pueblos, will help deter the erosive effects on the wall. As water is a rare resource in the Southwest, consider how it might be productively used, by diverting to irrigation or storage in rain barrels or cisterns. If cisterns are planned, make sure that any overflow will drain away from the building. Water can be retrieved from the cistern by gravity siphoning, if the topography allows, or may be pumped up with an inex-

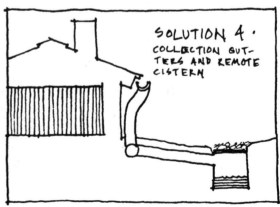

SOLUTION 4.
COLLECTION GUT-
TERS AND REMOTE
CISTERN

pensive hand pump. As a roof of 1500 square feet, in an area of average annual precipitation of only 13 inches, will collect 13,000 gallons per year, this is a resource which is wisely put to productive use. While probably not suitable for drinking, roof water used in irrigation will definitely conserve on water bills.

In the case of overhanging, continuous eaves — either on flat or pitched roofs — gutters may not have been included in the original construction, but can usually be added without considerable impact to the building's historic appearance, if done properly. Again, as water is collected at downspouts, make sure it is safely diverted from the building, or consider its storage or productive use.

Problem 3:
Cracks, Tilting & Bulging:
Structural Problems
Most old adobe buildings that survive in

reasonable condition were well sited and carefully built to begin with. However, structural problems may develop over time — due to the perpetual nemeses of moisture, differential settling, excessive bearing, thermal expansion and contraction, or incompatible materials.

Though cracks, tilting and bulging may be quite visible — particularly in mud plaster buildings — their cause is often difficult to diagnose. In an unpublished report on adobe preservation, developed at the University of Arizona (see Bibliography), general symptoms and possible causes were suggested. These have been represented graphically in the accompanying chart.

It is critical to observe changes over time in the structural condition of any adobe building. Some settling of the structure generally will have occurred during and imme-

STRUCTURAL PROBLEMS IN ADOBE WALLS

Appearance:	Condition:	Probable cause:	General remedy.
	Short hairline cracks throughout surface	Shrinkage of material in drying	Not a serious problem: renew plaster to prevent water from entering wall
	Cracks between adobe and other material	Separation of elements due to stress, moisture, thermal contraction	Fill cracks with adobe; patch
	Vertical or zig-zag cracks in long wall, at corner or opening	Shrinkage after thermal expansion	Cracks may be filled and patched, but check for moisture in wall, as this probably relates to problem
	Symetrical cracks sloping up and away from both sides of a wall opening	Wall rupture due to excessive load	Additional support needed, structural column may be helpful; see a professional
	Bulging	Adobe erosion or foundation settling	Address water problem, measure moisture; shore up with adobe banco or buttress; see a professional
	Vertical or sloping cracks with evidence of slippage	Foundation settling or stress of uneven loading	Spot patching, shoring of foundation, or regrading if condition is stable; otherwise, see a professional
	Tilting	Foundation settling	Push wall back into place with shoring, fill cracks; see a professional
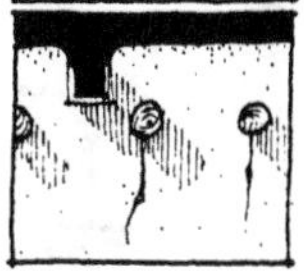	Wall fractures due to poorly distributed point loading	Excessive loads, absence of adequate bond beam	See a professional

'Control Unit' at the Ghost Ranch Sundwellings Demonstration Center: essentially a regional-type adobe building, employing simple native construction features; and 28% effective in passive solar space heating performance! The sloping sections flanking the door are solar hot water collectors.

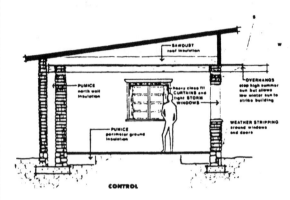

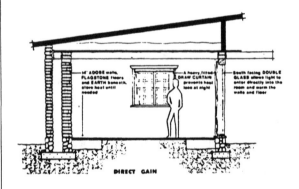

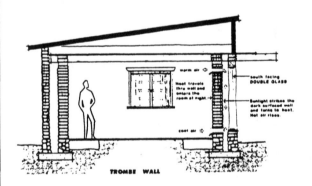

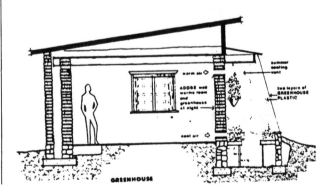

diately after construction, but it may continue on a periodic long-term basis. A stable crack may not be serious, but one that shows signs of movement probably indicates a more serious structural problem. If this is the case, there is a limited amount of work that can be done safely without some consultation with a specialist.

ENERGY AND THE ADOBE WALL

Though adobe is actually rather poor in insulative quality, its mass creates an effective heat storage medium, thereby increasing the thermal stability of the building. This makes the Southwest's older, uninsulated but heated adobe structures fairly comfortable year-round. This is borne out by adobe buildings throughout the world, almost none of which are 'insulated' in the modern sense of the word. Just the same, when an adobe building gets very cold in the winter, it can take a long time to reheat. The optimum thickness of the passive solar collecting and radiating adobe wall has been the subject of a great deal of conjecture, research, and data. Existing evidence suggests that optimal thickness varies from 14 inches on the south, to more than three feet on the north, when building with uninsulated adobe.

The Sundwellings Demonstration Center at Ghost Ranch near Abiquiu, New Mexico, was designed in the mid 1970s to test and demonstrate three distinct applications of passive solar technology — direct gain, trombe wall, and greenhouse — combined with indigenous, 'low-tech' adobe buildings. A control building with conventional fenestration in doors and windows was included. All buildings

Comparative sections of the four Sundwellings buildings, demonstrating the ready application of passive solar elements to the region's high-mass native adobe structures. (Adapted from Peter van Dresser's Homegrown Sundwellings)

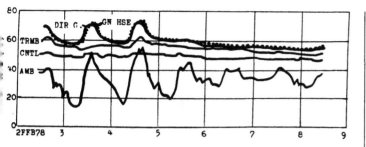

This graph illustrates unheated thermal performance of the four Sundwellings demonstration units, over a week's time in early February, 1978.

Note in particular, the line AMB is for ambient outdoor temperatures; the line above it, CNTL, is for the interior temperature of the control unit — with few specific 'energy' features other than good roof insulation and a north cavity wall. The 'control' line flattens out to a more or less stable temperature (warmer than outside), demonstrating the solar-absorptive and mass-storage capabilities of adobe. (Quentin Wilson, New Mexico Solar Energy Association Bulletin, Vol. 3, No. 6, June 1978)

had 14" adobe walls, a double north cavity wall and well insulated roof. Interestingly, the control building actually produced an effective passive solar performance of approximately 28%. (Quentin Wilson, New Mexico Solar Energy Association Bulletin.) This was due to the inherent capability of well-constructed traditional earth buildings to collect, store, and distribute the Southwest's intense solar radiation.

Problem 4:
Heat Loss through an Adobe Wall

Solution A:
Add Insulation

Contemporary construction practice with adobe usually includes exterior insulation, and this may be considered as a retrofit for historic buildings. One inch of polystyrene insulation over a 14 inch adobe wall, with ¾ inch stucco, increases it thermal resistance from R13 to R22: almost twice as much. (New Mexico Research and Development Institute) Exterior insulation captures the mass of the wall within the thermal envelope, but it will also trap water at the interface of materials, as it condenses on the warm side of impervious surfaces (just as water beads form on the outside of an iced drink glass on a hot summer day).

If walls are already well dried, and no substantial amount of vapor is being generated within, this may be a suitable solution. But, as this is a relatively new practice, only continued observation of existing buildings will tell if it is really wise for historic adobe buildings. Both rigid panels and blown foams are used, but the former produces a flat effect rather out of character with many old

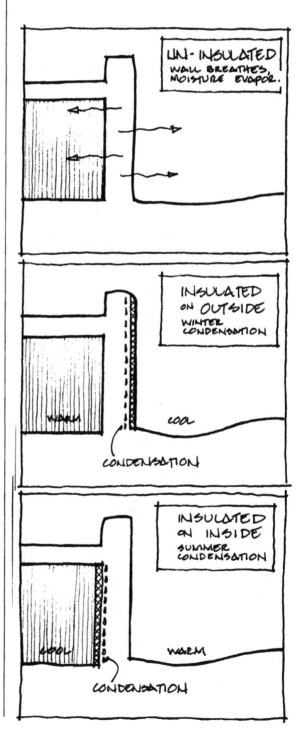

INSULATING AN ADOBE WALL
Insulating adobe walls — particularly walls on other than south exposures — improves their thermal performance. Problems, however, can occur in high humidity situations.

The most common contemporary practice is to place insulation on the exterior, isolating the adobe mass within the thermal envelope.

105

buildings, particularly those in the more supple puebloid styles. Walls may also be insulated on the interior — but this isolates the storage mass outside, where it does less good. It also uses up valuable interior space and is seldom done.

When insulation is added, existing wood trim frames on doors and windows have to be removed, and the casing deepened, before they are re-installed on the new surface. Leaving them in place, with the new wall bulging away from their now-recessed position, may work for Pueblo Revival (where there is little trim of this sort anyway), but it is unwise and unsightly as visited upon most other styles.

With exterior insulation, interior walls of rooms which generate a fair amount of moisture — such as bathrooms and kitchens — may be painted with an oil-based paint, to condense water before it enters the wall. Low sheen enamels are available which are more compatible with most historic interiors.

Solution B:
Do Not Add Insulation
Addition of insulation to either the interior or exterior walls of an historic adobe building may be detrimental to its character, and may cause water-related structural problems. As heat losses and gains through walls represent a relatively modest percentage of the energy load of adobe buildings — consider, instead, attention to the roof and windows, where losses and gains are greater. Also modifications here are likely to have less impact on the appearance of the building.

Solution C:
Color Treatment
Color can affect the thermal performance of a high-mass wall considerably. This is why the solar-adobe trombe wall is always dark in color, beneath its glazed covering. If south walls are light, consider coloring them darker (within reason, of course — black would be in wretched taste almost anywhere!).

A bit technical, but of some interest: the ASHRAE 'steady state' R value (thermal resistance) of a 10'' adobe wall, with ¾'' stucco, is R4 — very low. Taking into account the climatic character of the more temperate Southwest, the New Mexico Research and Development Institute assigns the same wall an R10 — for a dark-colored, south facing adobe wall in Santa Fe. Better than twice as effective in actual performance!

Solution D:
Interior Design
In remodeling, closets, bookshelves, cabinetwork and other built-ins placed against north walls are effective ways of providing insulation, while facilitating the functional updating of the structure. If there is a choice, this is where they should go.

CHAPTER 9

ROOFS

In mountain areas, the benefits of a pitched roof were recognized as quickly as the materials to build them became available. Here, significant deterioration reveals an earlier sawn-board roof beneath a later sheathing of corrugated metal.

In restoration, the board sheathing would make a fascinating, if somewhat problematic solution, because they are quite rare now — a sort of 'museum piece.' However, combined with modern asphalt-based sheathing beneath, and wood preservative oils, it would be possible to produce a beautifully historic roof which is also water-tight.

Flat earth roof construction in the Southwest followed the same basic formula, developed by early Puebloan cultures by A.D. 600, up until the mid 19th century. This heavy-mass roof, built of horizontal wood structure covered with adobe, is virtually identical to roof types traditionally employed in many other areas of the world and used as early as 8000 B.C. in Mesopotamia.

Early Spanish settlers made few significant changes in the Indians' traditional technology of roof construction, though artistic elaborations such as hewn, carved and polychromed wood members were introduced into monumental architecture, particularly mission churches. Later, adobe and fired masonry vaults, domes, and arches appeared with missions in Texas, Arizona, and California, together with pitched tile roofs.

The typical flat, parapetted roof of historic regional architecture is constructed in the following manner: peeled logs, called *vigas*, are laid onto the wall, sometimes on wooden bond beams which distribute their weight more evenly. Typical spacing is 1½ to 2½ feet These major spanning members are usually pine, particularly the straight and sturdy Ponderosa, but might be another wood, depending on what was locally available.

Between the vigas, or squared beams occasionally, wooden stick-work is placed. Called *latillas* if executed in round-section stock — often aspen — this decking was sometimes substituted with split cedar *cedros*, short adzed slabs called *tablas*, willow branches, coarse brush or other available wood. When milled lumber became available in the region, decks were increasingly made of sawn planks. Twigs or plant fibers, and later fabric, were laid over

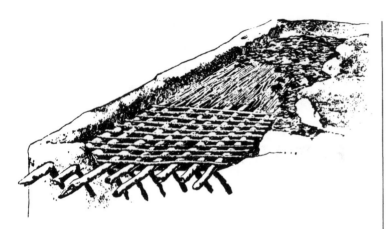

the deck for insulation and to prevent earth from sifting down; for on top of this prepared structure was laid 6 or more inches of compacted earth, with final coats of adobe plaster laid on top, as a water-resistant finish of sorts.

In early Indian and Spanish structures, there was customarily no separate ceiling structure. The underside of this layered wooden construction became the finished ceiling. Later examples sometimes added a second, dropped structure for the ceiling, creating a valuable insulating air space between the two. Often, this was simply a layer of sizing-stiffened cloth, attached to the vigas.

Roofs were usually framed around on three or four sides by parapet walls or *pendales* and sloped gradually toward water spouts called *canales*, which projected through the parapet. Canales were made of hollowed log sections, stone or pottery, and later, milled lumber assemblies, or just about anything that was handy and suitable. Occasionally, the parapet wall was left off one edge of the roof, and a shallow eave provided the same function — without some of the maintenance problems — as the canales: throwing roof water away from the vulnerable base and surface of the adobe walls. Stone was sometimes used as a cap on Indian pueblo and perhaps Spanish walls, to inhibit erosion at the top and retain the earth roof covering. With the establishment of brick kilns around 1850, the Territorial style brought an adapted cap to the parapet wall, as a denticulated (toothed) cornice of

brick, in regionalized Greek Revival style.

While some roofs from the mid 1800s had been constructed with pitched, opposing faces of sawn boards in lap pattern, the railroad brought wooden shingles and shakes, corrugated, standing seam and terne plate metal, and later, asphalt roofing and tile. As various architectural styles now proliferated, roof forms appropriate to each — hipped, gabled, mansard, and so forth — now took shape with the new surfacing materials. Rafter and truss systems of milled lumber — and on more primitive structures, peeled logs — supported these pitched roofs. Frequently, the pitched roof was added directly over an existing flat earth roof, providing for high thermal mass, an insulating air space, storage room, and a good weather-resistant finish.

Though pitched roofs caught on quickly, especially among the pragmatic vernacular builders of rural areas — more concerned with durable shelter than with style — flat roofs enjoyed a revival after the first decade of the 20th century in structures of deliberated architectural regionalism. These usually employed a more up-to-date, conventional built-up roofing surface: lower in mass than earth, but far more effective in shedding water. Although equally evident in other regions of the West, the pitched metal roof has become as much a part of the historic vernacular here as the flat roof, and many beautiful examples of post-Territorial buildings contain this feature.

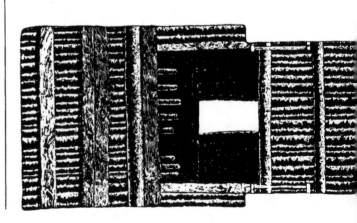

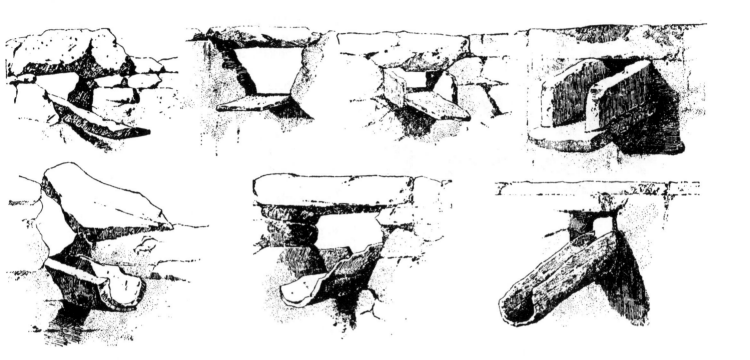

GENERAL OVERVIEW OF PROBLEMS WITH TRADITIONAL ROOFS

The two principal problems with roofs of all types are: keeping water out and keeping heat in. With the native tradition of flat parapetted roofs, water is a perennial preservation problem, especially as it can cause serious damage to the entire building. In terms of conservation, excessive heat loss is the primary consideration. Both flat and pitched roofs are examined here, with the emphasis on the region's hallmark flat, parapetted constructions. First preservation problems are addres-

Canales, or rain spouts, were used in the Indian pueblos and Spanish towns alike, to drain flat earth roofs — throwing water away from the vulnerable walls. These examples from Hopi and Zuni are of stone, except the last, which is of wood. (Victor and Cosmos Mindeleff, BAE Eighth Annual Report, 1891)

sed, and then a section follows which outlines solutions to conservation problems, specifically insulation. Construction addressing either preservation or conservation is likely to be affected by, or to benefit from attention to the other, so consider both when addressing any roof work.

Indians and Spaniards both occasionally made roofs of continuous logs, though their use is very limited — generally restricted to heavily timbered areas. This roof is from the Spanish Colonial reconstruction at Rancho de las Golondrinas.

Pitched roofs with lapped boards became popular in highland areas after the introduction of sawmills, in the 1850s.

109

ELEVATION 1 ELEV. 5705'

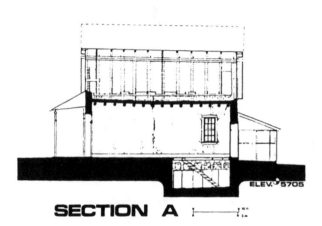

SECTION A ELEV. 5705

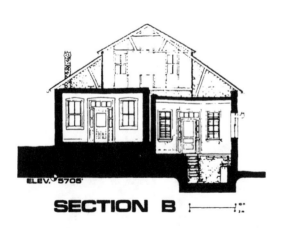

ELEV. 5705'

SECTION B

Elevation and sections of the Watson house in Lincoln, New Mexico. This whole unorthodox construction bridges two flat-roofed buildings — on different levels — with one wood-raftered roof, retaining existing viga-and-earth roofs below. (Architect's Atelier, for the Museum of New Mexico, State Monuments Division)

PRESERVATION PROBLEMS: FLAT ROOFS

The flat earth roof, for all of its native charm and effective storage mass, has always been a maintenance problem. Water can pool causing bearing problems, and is a perpetual hazard at canales and parapet walls. While many older earth roofs have been adapted to modern roofing materials of felt, petroleum derivatives and crushed rock — the built-up roof — these are seldom sound for more than 15 years before repairs must be done. All roofing materials have a limited life span. Keeping water off is the key to a sound adobe building, so the roof might be considered top priority in any preservation efforts.

Problem 1:
Unsound, Rotting or Sagging Wood Structure

Solution A:
Repair

Orignal structural materials should be maintained whenever possible, especially if exposed beams are of the less common square, hand-adzed type. If significant sagging is apparent, causing water to pool on the roof, replacement or additional interior support in the form of 'collector' beams may be necessary.

Vigas projecting through the walls visible on the exterior are part of the regional tradition, and are striking as their shadows modulate wall surfaces through the day. But they are inevitably prone to rot, seeping water to the interior and into adobe walls. The top side of the exposed vigas can be covered with fiberglass-reinforced tar, or fitted with metal flashings without considerable aesthetic impact, provided it is done with care. Severely rotted projecting vigas are probably best removed to not more than one-third their depth in the wall (from the exterior), and replaced with replica pieces which are mortised or dowelled into the solid section of the existing wood. Take special care to patch plaster and weather seal around them. Vigas must be solidly seated in the walls. Minor wall cracks may be patched with adobe, following the guidelines set down in Chapter 8 on Walls. Other considerations of bearing are also addressed in that chapter.

Epoxy resins may be used to fortify deteriorated wood sections, especially where structural bearing is not a serous consideration Information on the technique is included in Chapter 10, on Woodwork and Porches.

110

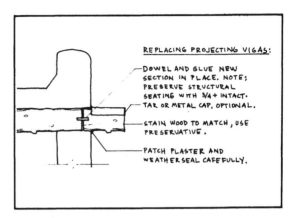

Projecting roof beams — or vigas — are very prone to rotting. The condition is evident here on the Hewett house in Santa Fe, a Territorial-period building which received a 'regionalizing' facelift in the early 20th century. Metal caps on the top side can help molify the inevitable problem, without significant impact on the appearance of the building.

Cutting off rotted projecting vigas, and plastering over the cut, is fairly common practice. It is certainly not recommended however, for projecting vigas lend a great deal of character to regional buildings — especially those of the Indian pueblos and the Pueblo Revival. Instead, consider repair patching, or their replacement in this manner.

Sometimes — particularly in the Pueblo Revival — buildings of architectural integrity otherwise, employed surface-attached projecting vigas for stylistic effect, as in the 1919 Museum of Fine Arts in Santa Fe. In this case, remove them as far as the original seating for replacement.

Solution B:
Replacement

If only a few of the vigas are rotted, cracked or seriously sagging, they can be replaced singly, but this is a rather specialized job and requires considerable skill. An experienced professional should be consulted.

If the entire roof is to be replaced, materials from the original should be reused when solid enough; and all new materials should duplicate the original as closely as possible in appeareance. Sometimes roof beams — if sagging but basically solid — are simply turned over, reversing the bow from downward to upward. Structural decks of reinforced lightweight ferroconcrete have been

TRADITIONAL ROOF CONSTRUCTION
1. *Peeled-log vigas*
2. *Latillas, cedros or adzed tablas*
3. *Twigs and brush*
4. *Compacted adobe*

CONTEMPORARY ROOF CONSTRUCTION
1. *Sawn beams or vigas*
2. *Milled lumber or traditional decking*
3. *Vapor barrier*
4. *Rigid insulation*
5. *Pumice, raked slope to canales*
6. *Plywood rigid decking*
7. *Built-up roofing with gravel on top*
8. *Metal flashings*

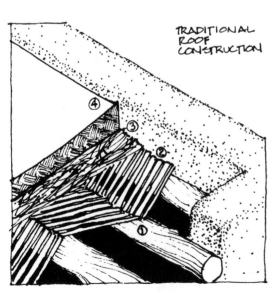

successfully employed in some extensive re-habilitations. In constructing a new roof, consider in particular the criteria of insulation and venting laid out later in this chapter.

Especially where a high parapet wall will hide the change in depth, a new insulated and vented roof of simple joist construction may be laid over the existing roof. The additional weight must be carefully considered in evaluating the bearing capacity of the walls and existing roof.

Problem 2:
Water Leaking or Seeping into Structure

Water is the worst enemy of adobe buildings. Aside from the obvious inconvenience to inhabitants, water leaking into adobe walls can cause serious structural damage. One of the principal keys to preserving an adobe building is a good roof; without it the walls may eventually be damaged beyond repair.

Solution A:
Repair of the Flat Roof

To seal leaks in an earth roof, the traditional method is a fresh coat of adobe plaster. Still, the mud finish is not watertight, and it will absorb moisture during extended periods of precipitation. After a heavy snow, one still sees Taos Pueblo residents shoveling snow from the earth roofs of their terraced houses. As the earth gets wet it also increases in weight, and this can cause bearing problems in the roof members and walls. Additional coats of adobe plaster will gradually add to the load of the roof. Especially if the roof is already showing signs of sagging, some of the existing adobe layers must be stripped away before applying additional coats.

If the original earth roof has already been sheathed with built-up roofing or asphalt roll material, this too will require occasional maintenance and replacement about every 15 years. This is a fairly standard procedure, but care must be taken to provide a watertight membrane in all seamed areas.

Canales, parapet flashings, chimneys and vents protruding through the roof are especially prone to leaking. Care must be taken to assure that all flashings are continuously sealed, and run at least 7″ vertically and 5″ tightly beneath the roofing material. A common practice among roofers is to run roll-type roofing material up the parapet wall; but it is only a matter of time before thermal expansion — or worse yet, ice or hail — causes cracking at this vulnerable corner. A much better and far more permanent, if somewhat more expensive solution, incorporates metal flashings at these critical areas. Good instructions for flashing repair can be found in *Readers Digest Complete Do-it-yourself Manual*, and other resources listed in the Bibliography.

Solution B:
Replacement

Roof replacement due to structural considerations has been covered in the preceding section, but if replacement of roofing is required only for purposes of watertightness, the work will be much easier A built-up roof may be recoated by a professional roofer. Small crushed gravel must be laid over the top to reflect summer heat and reduce ultra-violet deterioration of the petroleum sealants. All flashings should be carefully checked. Asphalt roll material can be applied at pitches greater than 1″ per foot, for a somewhat lower cost. Seamed metal applications may be made on pitches greater than 2″ per foot. As in all preservation choices, every effort should be made to duplicate original materials. In the case of an actual earth-surfaced roof, its reconstruction would, in most situations, represent the obsessions of an historic purist, for better water-proofing materials are now available.

For the condition of an earth roof to be replaced by a ferroconcrete deck, earth can be replaced over the finished and sealed deck to recreate the appearance, while avoiding some of the maintenance problems of an all-adobe roof. (This was done in reconstruction work in the Hopi town of Walpi in the late 1970s with considerable success.) For flat roofs, subject to the greatest solar exposure during the summer months, light-colored or reflective finishes are generally to be preferred to darker colors.

Most flat roof finishes, including built-up roofing, are not made to be walked on, as this will eventually cause leaks. Just the same, use of the flat roof as seasonal outdoor space is both pleasant and in keeping with its historic function — allowing realization of its inherent character. If this is intended, bearing capacity of the roof structure must be analyzed first. Decks of wood may be laid upon safely supported roofs, taking care to avoid damage to the weatherproofing material beneath. Hard surfaces of tile or brick are nice, but are heavy and must be properly supported, flashed and drained.

PRESERVATION PROBLEMS: PITCHED ROOFS

Approaching preservation and conservation issues with pitched roofs is much more routine than with flat roofs. Other sourcebooks contain a substantial amount of good material, but general guidelines are briefly mentioned here, as they bear upon a number of the Southwest's historic structures. The most distinctive regional pitched roof is probably seen here in the Mountain Gabled style (see Chapter 5), though it appears in a wide variety of other styles as well.

Problem 3:
General Deterioration

Solution:
Basic Preservation and Restoration

Preservation is generally a matter of sealing, nailing down, patching or spot replacement of parts. New metal can be glaze-rubbed, painted or oxidized to match existing material. Often salvage materials can be found in the area, and if these date from a similar construction period, will probably have developed a compatible patina or aged appearance. Bright, new shingy galvanized metal usually looks inappropriate, whether in patched areas only, or for entire roofs on historic buildings, and new finishes take a long time to mellow, so they may benefit from some creative assistance.

Any distinguishing roof details (such as at ridge or eave) should certainly be preserved or restored. The addition of gutters, often a wise idea, is discussed later in this chapter. In some areas — New Mexico's Belen and Tierra Amarilla come to mind — ambitious frontier salesmen make their mark apparent in pervasive

The San Juan Church in historic Lincoln, New Mexico, center of the ranchers-versus-farmers Lincoln County War of the late 19th century. Simple neo-Greek Territorial pediments over the windows combine with a pitched metal roof: signature features of the Mountain Gabled style. (Architects Atelier, for the Museum of New Mexico, State Monuments Division)

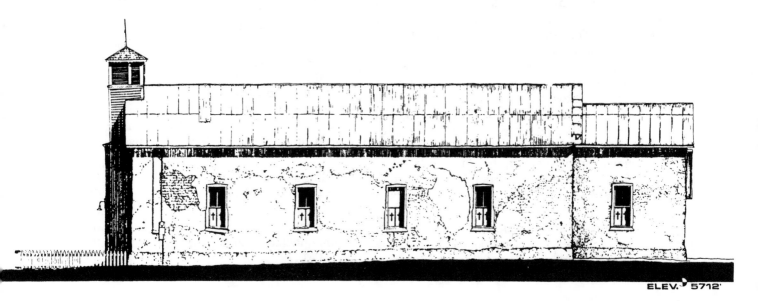

ELEV. 5712'

Pitched metal roofs are part of the rural vernacular in architecture throughout the Southwest. Damaged or missing sections, as seen here, can usually be replaced with old material which has developed a similar patina — or new material can be chemically oxidized or stained to match.

localized detail features, such as the ornamental ridge finial and lightening rod. Keep them; replace them where missing; and in no case sell them to antique dealers. They can buy reproductions more conveniently and less expensively than the average homeowner.

Never do any major roof repairs without seriously considering the benefits of adding or upgrading insulation. This is usually a relatively easy matter with pitched roofs, and some evaluation on the subject follows.

ENERGY AND THE TRADITIONAL SOUTHWESTERN ROOF

The flat, heavy earth roof of traditional native construction is reasonably well-suited to this region's climate. Not surprisingly, other areas of the planet with similar climate — the steppes of Afghanistan or the plains and Atlas Mountains of Morocco, for example — tend to produce similar types of roof construction.

With wide fluctuations of day-to-night temperatures, a mass material like adobe can absorb heat during the day, keeping interiors cooler, and radiate it at night, warming the spaces. This stabilizing time lag feature has been known to be a factor in the comfort of adobe buildings for a long time, and it works for roofs as well as for walls. The graph on page 115 shows how extremes of temperature are moderated by the mass of the roof, and how the time lag of heat transfer enhances comfort for both day and night. The graph is shown for the summer, though a similar effect of collection and distribution may be noted in the walls during the winter (more perpendicular to the sun's angle at that time).

Intense solar radiation produces enough warmth for daytime activities outdoors during much of the winter. Especially with protective massing on the north side, as at Mesa Verde or

Acoma Pueblo, flat roofs become effective extensions of indoor living space, expanding architectural function from shelter and climate moderating mass to usable floor space as well.

When pitched roofs became popular after 1880, the insulating factor of a dead-air space was introduced. Added directly over existing adobe roofs, the benefits of both mass and insulation could be employed. If an existing earth roof had been removed, or in new construction where it was not originally included, at least the benefit of the insulating space and the erosion deterent of projecting eaves could be enjoyed, effectively shading the structure during the high sun of summer months, but allowing the low winter sun to fall on the adobe walls.

In the uncommon circumstance where interior spaces rise the full interior height of the pitched roof, not only is the volume of air to be heated much larger, but heat stratification will naturally collect the warmest air at the top, where it is less useful. The larger surface — often twice as large as the flat roof for typical pitches — may also lose heat at twice the rate. It is not surprising that relatively few cathedral ceilings exist in historic buildings in the Southwest, though the technology to create them existed. Attic spaces are customarily not finished and used only as storage.

In a typical home in New Mexico, more than one fourth of all heat loss occurs through the ceiling and roof. Heat loss occurs in two ways. The first is heat loss due to poor insulation. The second is due to direct convection through openings in the roof, such as undampered chimneys, gravity relief vents, exhaust fans, loose fitting construction, and so on. The roof-related breakdown of heat loss for the average house, as published by the Public Service Company of New Mexico, shows:

Ceiling and roof due to poor insulation	12.8%
Vent-a-hood over range	6.0%
Fireplace	6.0%
Bathroom vent	1.0%
Other (including some wall infiltration)	2.0%
TOTAL	27.8%

By contrast, heat loss due to window and door infiltration averages 13% of the total; heat loss due to poor wall insulation averages 15.2%. Thus, next to heating and cooling equipment maintenance, the roof and ceiling should receive the highest priority in most conservation efforts. From a preservation point of view, remedial work at the roof and ceiling are least likely to affect the historic character of the building. Considering the cost and visual impact, probably the two most effective areas to save energy are with good roof insulation and well-designed storm windows and doors.

A most important consideration when insulating roofs is moisture condensation. Even though many parts of the Southwest are arid in climate, the average home generates 25 pounds of water per day: a total of about 250 gallons during the heating season. This warm, moist air rises within the living space. As it cools on contact with cold attic or roof surfaces, the water vapor condenses on these surfaces, much like moisture condenses on a cold glass of water on a summer day. If the condensation occurs in spaces which are not ventilated to allow evaporation, dry rot — a type of fungus — can infect the building's wooden members. There are four conditions for dry rot to thrive: (1) moisture; (2) darkness; (3) wood for food; and (4) temperatures above 50°F. Just as bad, the moisture can condense within the insulation if it is not properly laid, with a vapor barrier on the warm side to keep the moisture out. If this happens, the R-value of the insulation drops dramatically. Thus, keep

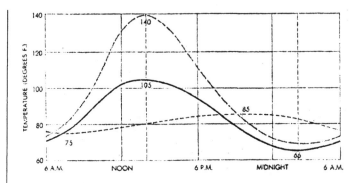

ADOBE HOUSE & ROOF TEMPERATURES, Summer
Roof Surface — — — — — — — — — — —
Outside temperature ——————————
Inside temperature ··

This graph shows the capacity of a high-mass earth roof to moderate the extremes of summer temperature. Heat is absorbed during the day, keeping the interior cool, and is re-radiated at night, into the room and (substantially) back into the sky.

Flat earth roofs of the type found in traditional Southwestern architecture have been built by man for at least 8,000 years; and they appear with notable frequency historically in culturally disconnected areas where the climate is hot or temperate, and dry. (James Marston Fitch and Daniel P. Branch, "Primitive Architecture and Climate," Scientific American, December 1960)

in mind the dangers of neglecting moisture control when insulating an older building.

Problem 4:
Excessive Loss of Heated Air through Cracks in Loose-Fitting Construction, Vents, and Other Openings
Early Indian, Spanish, and Territorial buildings were, as a rule, plagued by imprecisely fitting seams and joints. Aggravated by the natural weathering process, this necessitated a continual filling of cracks and chinking of crevices — especially before each winter — to deter loss of heated air through roofs, chimneys, around windows and doors. Most historic buildings have been further opened to heat loss by the later addition of appliance vents and holes for electrical and plumbing runs.

Solution A:
Fill Holes in Roof and Ceiling
Where Heated Air Can Escape
Check all attic spaces and if possible, ceiling plenums for openings that can be sealed off. Look for rays of sunlight and water stains on the rafters or roof sheathing. Check for spaces around electrical conduit and plumbing and for cracks between planks and where the

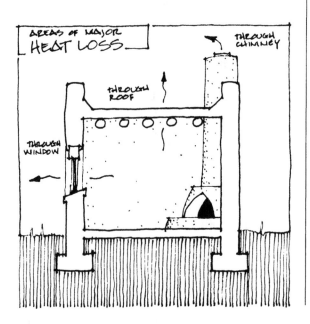

115

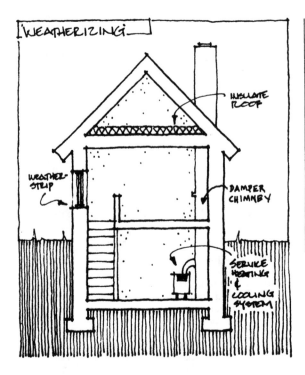

WEATHERIZING

INSULATE ROOF

WEATHER STRIP

DAMPER CHIMNEY

SERVICE HEATING & COOLING SYSTEM

wall meets the roof. These spaces can be filled with caulking, insulating spray foam or chinked with bits of batt insulation. Do not block off attic or plenum vents; otherwise, excessive moisture will be trapped and cause deterioration of wood and moisture-prone members.

The free vent area should be about 1/300 of the ceiling area below. If excessive water condensation is noticed in the attic during the winter, the installation of a small electric or wind turbine fan will help draw out the moisture-laden air, as well as assisting in summer cooling. Install these devices in a manner which is unobtrusive to the primary elevations of the building.

Solution B:
Install Dampers and
Provide Outside Combustion Air

Many historic buildings have been converted from fireplaces — or coal, wood, or oil-burning heaters — to gas or propane furnaces. If the furnace is drawing combustion air from *heated* spaces, then during idle firing periods, heated room air is escaping up the vent. If this is so, then installing a vent damper would be a cost-effective retrofit, and will not affect the building's architectural integrity. These devices are installed within the vent, and close it off either electronically (when the gas flow ceases), or thermostatically (when the flue gas temperature drops below a predetermined setting). The electronic damper is usually

available only for electronically ignited furnaces as opposed to those with standing pilot lights. The total cost is presently between $60 and $100 per flue with installation.

The fireplace is also, paradoxically, a source of heat loss in most houses. Dampers are imperative. Though many old fireplaces did not have them, they can be installed without any significant visual impact.

To make a fire, air is needed for combustion. Logically, it is better not to use the air from inside the building, which is already heated. For some furnaces and all fireplaces, the best thing to do is provide fresh, unheated air from outside. Ducting it in may require some planning, but it can usually be worked out. Wood stoves are available which have this feature built in.

Problem 5:
Excessive Heat Loss through Roof
Due to Inadequate Insulation

Solution A:
Retrofitting A Flat Roof with Insulation

There are a variety of ways in which a flat roof can be retrofitted with insulation, and the specific choice will depend upon the particular characteristics of the building's construction — such as the existing condition and materials of the roof, and the height of parapet walls and their ability to conceal additional construction. Several approaches are illustrated here.

Of paramount concern in each is the location of a vapor barrier. As stated earlier, warm air will tend to condense its water content on a cold surface, so the placement of a vapor barrier, or appropriate venting of the moist air, is essential to each solution. If water is condensing within an existing earth roof, like walls, it will eventually turn to mud, severely complicating preservation problems as the whole roof eventually sags under the additional loading. Some methods are clearly preferred to others, but the choice depends upon the particular construction characteristics of the roof.

Solution B:
Retrofitting A Pitched Roof With Insulation

Pitched roofs are generally an easier insulation retrofit than flat roofs, and it can be done with no aesthetic impact to the structure. Also, the following solutions C and D exploit the intrinsic characteristics of the south-sloping roof as a potential solar collector, but they should be well thought out first.

Typical existing earth roof, with five various strategies for insulation. Note the placement of the vapor barrier, and the probable location of condensation in each. For rooms other than kitchens and bathrooms, condensation may not be a problem.

TYPICAL EXISTING
Earth roof over planks, latillas, tablas, cedros etc.
No vapor barrier, water transpires easily. High mass but low insulation.

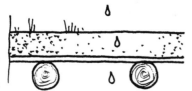

EARTH REMOVED
Rigid or blown foam with built-up roofing.
Vapor barrier inside
Good insulation but low mass.

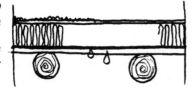

PUMICE OVER EXISTING EARTH
Built-up roofing over decking
Vapor barrier between: condensation in earth
No vapor barrier: condensation in insulation

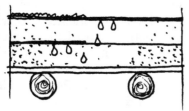

INSULATION FOAM OVER EARTH
Built-up roofing
Vapor barrier between: condensation in earth
Vapor barrier above: condensation in insulation

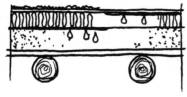

DECK RAISED ON PURLINS WITH VENTED CHASES
Vapor barrier down
Benefits from both mass and insulation, but a complex installation. Requires high parapets.

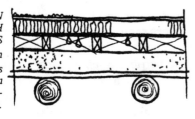

COVED CEILING
Insulation in cove space with vapor barrier down

The best place to locate insulation is where it will minimize the volume of space to be heated. While insulation between the roof-supporting rafters in the attic will certainly help, if the space is unused, the more efficient place is between ceiling joists, or over the existing attic floor. A vapor barrier must be placed toward the bottom — toward the warm space — and the attic space should be vented. Fiberglass batts may be used, or loose insulation may be raked in. To keep insulation away from electrical boxes, a tin can with the ends removed is an easily constructed shield. Distance of fill from the fixture should be at least 3 inches.

Cellulose (generally fire-proofed shredded newspaper) is the least expensive and popular of the loose fills, though vermiculite and pumice are also used. It may be wise to construct a walkway across the ceiling joists to prevent the classic (slap-stick, though genuinely hazardous) situation of stepping through the ceiling.

*INSULATING A
PITCHED ROOF*

Note: current practice suggests a total insulative value for roofs at around R40: about 12" of cellulose fill or fiberglass batts.

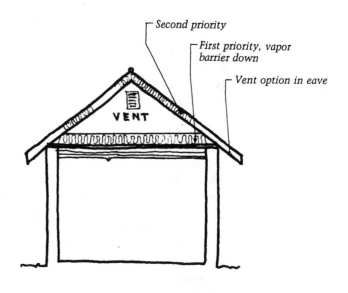

Second priority

First priority, vapor barrier down

Vent option in eave

VENT

117

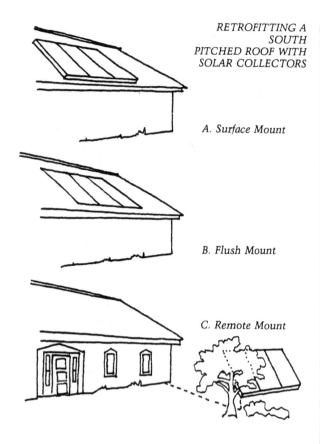

A. Surface Mount

B. Flush Mount

C. Remote Mount

This sort of solar collector might be used for either air or water heating. Especially for significant elevations, visible retrofits should be avoided.

GLAZED COLLECTORS, either for hot air of hot water.

A. The most expedient, but least desireable solutions: surface mounted collectors.

B. A more complex but less objectionable solution, not recommended for primary or public facades: the flush mounted collector.

C. Sometimes the best solution, especially where the roof is exposed to view or part of a significant elevation: remote collectors, screened from view; duct to structure.

*Problem 6:
How To Use The Pitched Roof
As A Solar Collector*

*Solution A:
Glazed Collector Retrofits*

Pitched roofs on historic buildings may, in some cases, be effectively uses as mounting surfaces for glazed, flat-plate solar collectors, for either space or water heating. Carefully consider the impact of these collectors on publicly visible or historically significant elevations. Generally, they are probably not a good idea, and would be better in a remote location, off the building.

Flush-fitting units, set into the roof depth, though more difficult to install and weather seal, would be preferrable in terms of visual impact to those which are mounted on the surface. Even if the roof pitch is not optimal for the collectors — and it probably isn't, for most roofs are not steep enough — it may be better to sacrifice some efficiency in order to avoid the disruptive appearance of weirdly tilted, disengaged hardware. The case study in Chapter 13 explores this and other options further.

*Solution B:
The Traditional Pitched Roof
As An Unglazed Collector*

Just as the pitched roof may constitute a significant portion of the heat loss surface of the building, it also represents an equivalent area of potential heat collection. Many typical regional buildings of adobe, with pitched metal roofs, are oriented so that a major part of the roof is exposed to the south, at vertical angles from 30 to 45° to the horizontal: rather good for solar collection. This is demonstrated by examples in the Penasco Valley of northern New Mexico, as illustrated in Chapter 5.

With no apparent change to the exterior this surface may — with appropriate retrofitting construction — be put to use as a large, unglazed flat-plate collector. Although the surface is often larger than the south facing walls themselves, the collection efficiency is much lower than glazed collectors, so miracles are not to be expected. But the installation cost is much lower too, and there is virtually no aesthetic impact.

The basic notion of this retrofit is based upon Peter and Florence van Dressers' simple observation: that uninsulated attics often get hot, even in the winter. Their idea was to use the vertical sloping space between the rafters on the south side as long collection channels. The north slope of the roof, and the underside of the channels are insulated, as shown in the diagram. Heat is collected as it rises to the apex, and ducted into the living space with a little fan support. Heat is stored in the mass of the building itself, or some form of specific storage medium, such as water cylinders or a rockbed (though low charging temperatures may not make specific storage mass worth the cost, effort, and space).

Efficiency is relatively low, and the system operates for only a few hours a day during the heating season. Heavy winds and resulting surface losses may make it inoperative altogether. Dampering must be provided to prevent back-siphoning, which would cool the building at night (though this could be an asset in the summer).

Although this simple, unglazed solar roof treatment was demonstrated on van Dresser's experimental house at El Rito in northern New Mexico, no exact data on efficiency has yet been collected. As of this writing, the New Mexico Solar Energy Association has planned some monitored retrofits and new construction incorporating this system. If results prove worth the modest investment, this retrofit could have a substantial impact on conservation in cool but sunny highlands, where high-pitched metal roofs are well represented among historic buildings.

Problem 7:
Water Wasted By Absence Of
Rain Gutter On A Pitched Roof

The majority of earlier historic structures with pitched roofs in the Southwest seem to have been built originally without rain gutters. In the eclectic period of the post-Railroad styles, together with other forms of trim, they became more prevalent; but deterioration may have predicated their removal. Water concentrated along the wall, as it drops from the eave, can cause damage to the wall, particularly if it is adobe. Certainly, it is a nuisance over the doorway. Likewise, water uncollected and unused is water wasted.

EXISTING EAVE & INSTALLING
AN EAVE GUTTER AND DRIP CAP

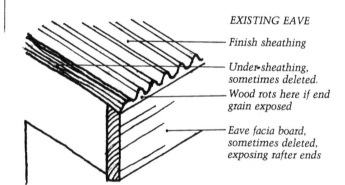

EXISTING EAVE
— *Finish sheathing*
— *Under-sheathing, sometimes deleted.*
— *Wood rots here if end grain exposed*
— *Eave facia board, sometimes deleted, exposing rafter ends*

AN UNGLAZED
COLLECTING ROOF

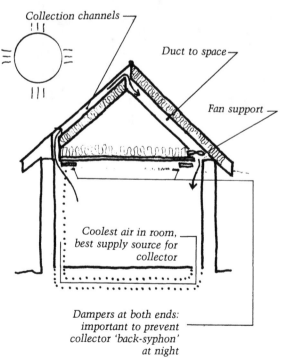

Collection channels

Duct to space

Fan support

Coolest air in room, best supply source for collector

Dampers at both ends: important to prevent collector 'back-syphon' at night

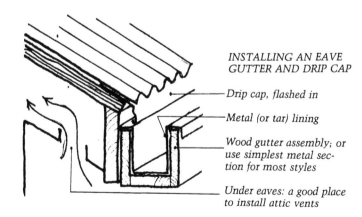

INSTALLING AN EAVE
GUTTER AND DRIP CAP

— *Drip cap, flashed in*
— *Metal (or tar) lining*
— *Wood gutter assembly; or use simplest metal section for most styles*
— *Under eaves: a good place to install attic vents*

Solution A:
Adding Rain Gutters

Although they may not have been historically present, rain gutters can be added to the eaves of a pitched roof without considerable impact on the appearance of the building. They can also be added along any projecting eaves of flat-roofed buildings. Snow sliding into them demands that they be securely attached. A drip cap along the edge of the finished roof will deter rotting of under-sheathing, rafter ends or eave fascia boards.

Standard metal gutters can be found, and the simplest available type is probably best for most regional historic styles. Paint them in the most unobtrusive color, probably the color of the roof or wall. Perhaps better for more rustic rural buildings, but more elaborate, is a built-up one-by wood section, which is lined with metal and/or roofing tar. Locate downspouts where least obtrusive probably around the corner from primary elevations, and paint them the color of the wall. Simple chain runways for the water — into a stone splash area — can also be used. The diversion and use of collected water is discussed in the preceding Chapter 8 on walls.

CHAPTER 10

PORCHES & WOODWORK

In pre-Spanish native Indian architecture, finish woodwork of all kinds was rare. The absence of metal tools made it quite difficult to hew wood into square sections, so most of what little one finds in earlier periods is, naturally, round. Just the same, archaeology has revealed that the Anasazi did dress wood into flatboards for roof decks, and with considerable precision — given the stone tools involved — into objects for ceremonial use.

Some wood details of native Puebloan architecture can be seen as preserved or restored at Acoma, Taos, and the Hopi towns. This includes ladders, lintels over doors and windows, twig grills in wall openings, and interior features such as the blanket bar on which household items, textiles and clothing could be hung. The porch, as one finds it most frequently today among Indians towns of the Southwest, is usually a free-standing shade structure, called a *ramada*, of vertical and horizontal poles with brush for the roof. Wooden galleries did exist historically in some Pueblos, such as Taos and Pecos, and these may be Spanish in inspiration.

With Spanish conquest came metal tools, though they were scarce, and precious. Some adzed and hewn wood appears at this time, but even until the 1840s it was relatively rare. Repeated use and sharpening of tools wore them down. It may be reasonable to suspect that the early tradition of cantilevered exterior vigas, projecting from the walls, may be due in part to the desire to cut the wood only once, in the field.

Early Spanish porches were usually made of round columns with squared lintels, carried often on carved decorative capitals, *zapatas* (usually referred to as corbels, though

Phoenix Ranch headquarters, 1864, one of a generation of great Territorial mansions in New Mexico. Here the Greek Revival detail is of exceptionally high caliber in design and execution.
(Museum of New Mexico Photo Archives)

technically they are not corbels unless they are engaged in the wall). Some of these historic capitals survive today, and are widely replicated and interpreted in Revival styles.

The Indian Pueblos also incorporated details of Spanish woodwork such as the column and capital ensemble, and pintled or puncheon type doors and window shutters. There remain very few and fragmentary examples of period pre-Columbian and Spanish Colonial woodwork. Particularly in the most truly monumental architecture of the period, the mission churches, examples of the original woodwork can be seen preserved, especially in entrance facades and altar panels. Some elaborations — like ceiling structures of hewn, carved and polychromed beam and corbel-work — are also seen, and are likewise copied in the Pueblo Revival.

During the Territorial period, after 1846, milled lumber became available with the construction of sawmills in Las Vegas, Watrous, Santa Fe and later, other areas. Now architecture was capable of a considerable degree of refinement, and under the frontier influence of the Greek Revival, classically-derived detail became widespread. Many earlier Spanish Colonial houses were now remodelled to include more modern doors and windows and sometimes a Neo-Greek porch.

References to Neoclassicism are widespread in the region's historic Territorial period buildings, if only in the most rudimentary form, such as the flat triangular window

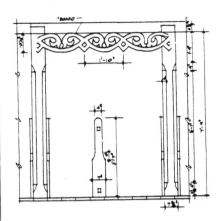

Detail of the portal of the Leandro Martinez house, Ranchitos de Taos, (no longer standing). Corners of the columns are cut away — chamfered — a detail typical of the Territorial period, perhaps suggesting roundness. The Carpenter Gothic trim board at the top is probably a later addition, reflecting post-Railroad Victorian influence. (Fort Burgwin Research Center, Southern Methodist University)

pediment. To be sure, most examples, especially earlier and those in more remote areas, were fairly primitive interpretations. But the style was capable of great refinement and 'correctness' in its use of the Classical orders, such as the fine detailing of the Quartermaster's Headquarters and other buildings at Fort Union, of the late 1860s (see Chapter 3).

With the arrival of the railroad, a multitude of architectural styles were introduced, and each had its own particular manner of porch and other woodwork. These ranged from Queen Anne to Italiannate Bracketed to Second Empire — the full Victorian spectrum. As these are not in the main vein of regional architecture, they are seldom addressed in the following examples. Preservation treatments specific to these various styles can be found in a number of references listed in the Bibliography. (However, the same basic rules hold: preserve original material wherever possible, and replicate where necessary.)

Portal from the Jose Gregorio Valdez house in Taos. This early 19th century Spanish Colonial house features a distinguishing portal, the main beam and zapatas of which are carved from one piece of wood — not altogether uncommon in the period.

Various other porch and woodworking details are also illustrated in Part I, Chapters 1-7. (Fort Burgwin Research Center, Southern Methodist University)

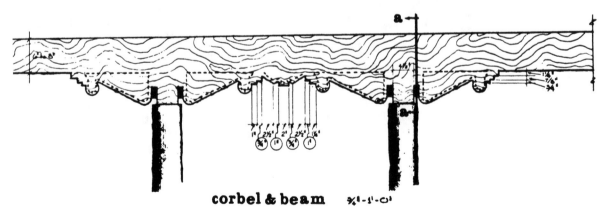

corbel & beam ¾"-1'-0'

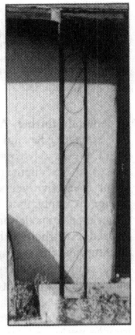

Porch post of the Strock house in Dixon, New Mexico 1984. In rural areas particularly, hand-crafted folk-Territorial details are still popular today — and a clear preference over the light weight "scrolled wrought iron" replacements often seen on older buildings: a dubiously "styled-up" retrofit which can only be regarded as kitsch.

With the Pueblo Revival style of the early 20th century, the broad undecorated massing of the traditional regional architecture was frequently visited with a more heavily encrusted detailing. Due, it seems, to the decorative tastes and more highly developed functional requirements of the times, woodwork became a more prominent feature than it ever had been in previous periods. This could include interior cabinetry; window, door and radiator grills; decorated and corbelled ceilings; a multitude of porch, colonnade and loggia configurations, and various other 'crafty' details.

GENERAL OVERVIEW OF
WOODWORK PRESERVATION

Most of the concerns with historic woodwork and porches in the Southwest are preservation and not energy conservation problems. Conservation problems and solutions are addressed more effectively in other components of the structure; however, a south or west porch, or protected entry, will have some bearing on the thermal performance of the structure. In any case, woodwork detail is often largely responsible for the architectural

Entrance porch of the Cuyler Preston House in Santa Fe. This important residence of the post-railroad era features some of the best Queen Anne style details to be found in the Southwest. Such fantasy was a significant departure from the cool austerity of the Territorial style; compare, for example the placement of a tremendously odd, but imaginative column at the corner, as opposed to the stately, if perhaps oppressive, colonnades of Fort Union (see page 40.)

character and historic interest of a building, and special care should be taken in its preservation or restoration.

Old buildings in this region have widely varying amounts of woodworking detail, dependent upon their period, style, degree of architectural savvy, and expense in construction. In general, all sound woodwork should be retained where possible, and given an appropriate treatment for preservation. Anything seriously deteriorated should be replicated, or replaced with materials as similar as possible to the original.

Water-related damage is the most typical problem with woodwork here, as it is everywhere. Because the Southwest is dryer than most areas, deterioration due to moisture is less a problem than in many other regions, which accounts in part for the abundance of solid (though often errantly maintained) historic buildings here. Just the same, intermittent periods of extreme heat and dryness, and cold and wet seasons, aggravate the relatively dry conditions somewhat. Certain regional styles — such as Pueblo Indian and Pueblo Revival — feature typical details like

projecting vigas and canales, which are especially vulnerable to moisture and other climatic stresses.

Preservation of historic woodwork is covered in a number of other more general sources, noted in the Bibliography. Problems and solutions explicit to particular Southwestern styles are addressed in the following section; but it would still be wise to consult some of the other, more comprehensive texts when working on wood elements of this region's historic buildings.

Problem 1:
Basic Maintenance & Preservation

Solution A:
Preservatives & Stains

Exterior woodwork in Spanish Colonial, Pueblo Indian, and various other styles is often left in a natural finish — perhaps inferring that nothing at all needs to be done to preserve it. This is not true: thanks to preservative oils, the wood can be encouraged to last much longer than it would untreated.

On old and dry wood, a preliminary coat should be applied, thinned 50% with turpentine or the appropriate solvent, encouraging it

to penetrate further. A second coat is applied full strength. Several brands of penetrating wood preservatives are available; Woodlife makes an excellent product which is used about every five years. It is toxic and some bother to apply, but well worth the effort. Other types of penetrating oils are more widely used; but, though they will extend the life and improve the appearance of wood, they are not technically preservatives. Just the same, they are definitely better than no treatment at all!

Wood preservatives and penetrating oils may be untinted ('natural'), or have pigments added, making them stains. If replica replacement pieces are used together with historic pieces, stains may be used to match the toning of the older wood. If restoration work includes more extensive new material, preservative stains will extend wood life and lend a more antique appearance, immediately.

Territorial woodwork from the Professor J.A. Wood house in Santa Fe, restored (and reconstructed) in the early 1980s. Woodwork in the Territorial era was often painted — usually white — and can be charming in its provincial rendition of the Greek Revival.

Garage doors of the Pueblo Revival, loosely interpreting the zaguan doors of the Spanish Colonial era. Instead of horse-drawn wagons entering the wide double-door entry, integral with the house, automobiles are parked within a structure isolated from the dwelling.

Solution B:
Paint

Painted woodwork may be repainted after the surface is clean of dust and dirt, old paint has been scraped and wire brushed, and necessary caulking and patching is done. Solve all problems of water, especially with respect to canales, gutters and downspouts, before painting. Careful preparation is the key to a good paint job, and extra effort here will definitely produce a superior and more durable result.

Oil-based paints provide the most attractive and lasting finish, and are best for old, dry wood. Latex paints are a clear second choice; but if latex paints have already been used, oil paint may not penetrate, and latex may have to be continued, or the old paint may have to be stripped. In the use of oil paints, a thin penetrating oil treatment may be applied a few weeks before repainting, to better preserve the wood. Old paint may be stripped entirely, either by sanding, water blasting or chemical strippers, all of which are usually worth the effort, but expensive and time-consuming. More complete information on the process for painting woodwork is contained among various home improvement and preservation books.

should be taken, as color forms one of the major visual features of the building. This is certainly the case if it is used sparingly against an adobe or earth-tone stucco wall (as it frequently is in the historic architecture of the Southwest). Paint may be chipped away in layers to reveal earlier or original colors. Original colors, when known, are probably the safest bet for restoration; they help bring out the particular historic character of the building.

Typical colors for woodwork in this region include shades of brown and grey-brown in the earlier styles, and white in the Territorial. Turquoise and other shades of blue have also been traditionally used, as well as certain dark or muted reds on occasion. Some local areas feature an historic use of very lively polychromes (several colors used together) — such as the turned-column Queen Anne porches of northern New Mexico's Tierra Amarilla. If the building has a roof which is visible, consider its color in selecting trim paint. In any case, the colors of the wall, wood trim and roof (if it is visible) should work well together.

The historic value of the structure will usually be enhanced by a traditional, rather than an adventuresome, approach to paint selection. Always consider the context in which the building exists: if other local buildings incorporate pastel blue for Territorial trim, and it appears to be an established tradition in the vicinity, it may be appropriate in restoration. Bear in mind that work on one building can affect popular tastes and subsequent developments in the neighborhood, favorably or unfavorably.

For buildings of other than regional style (such as those of the Railroad era), an entirely new palette of colors comes into play, and color selection among these styles — Queen Anne, Italianate, Victorian, Bungalow, and so on — can best be evaluated by referring to books related to those specific styles; however, consider the context in which the building exists. A Victorian house in a neighborhood dominated by Mediterranean and 'adobe' styles would look quite inappropriate in four shades of green and red, even though this might be historically correct for the style unto itself. This is not to be construed as an endorsement to paint everything in sight brown (though, sadly, it has often been done in Santa Fe). This only robs distinctive buildings of their character and original artistic integrity.

Solution C:
Caulking Damaged Wood

If minor, non-structural checking or cracking exists, caulking may be in order to

125

prevent water from entering. If the wood is to be painted, it is a relatively easy matter to cover the work. If however, the wood has a natural finish, a small amount of paint to match the wood-tone may be used. silicone caulking is clear, but creates a shiny surface. Vertical checking in Puebloid columns is common, and lends rustic character to the structure, so unless entering water appears to cause an advancing problem leave it as it is. Preservative attention is still the best treatment. More serious deterioration of woodwork is discussed in Problem 2.

Problem 2:
Deteriorated Wooden Members

As much of the Southwest's historic architecture features a similar building envelope of adobe, woodwork and porches often contribute prominently to the specific stylistic character. Over the years, buildings are put to many uses and abuses, so woodwork is often carved up, drilled out, or sawn off — to pass pipes, attach clothleslines or fences, or whatever. Likewise, water causes natural deterioration, and sometimes things get beyond basic preservation.

Solution A:
Patching

Holes or missing fragments of woodwork can be patched with infill pieces. Sections of corbelled capitals, for examples, may have broken off, and they can be replaced with pieces cut to replicate the missing sections, secured in place with pegs and glue. If adjacent wood is rotted, remove as much as necessary to reach solid material before patching. Retain original building fabric wherever possible, but when replacement of an entire component is necessary, read on.

Solution B:
Replacement & Reproduction

If building elements are seriously deteriorated or missing altogether, replica pieces can be fabricated to replace them. If any of the original material exists, study it to understand how it looks and how it is built. Moldings during the early Territorial period were made by hand with special molding planes, so don't expect to find them on the shelf at the building material supplier. They can be made in replica using hand or power tools (a friend of the author's takes great pleasure in fabricating his own, using his collection of antique tools!) or a reasonable facsimile might be found in commercial stock, though few suppliers have a very extensive selection. Retain original material wherever possible, if only in fragments.

Replacement of structural elements, such as columns, should follow the same general guidelines. Shoring to the desired finish level will be required, while the deteriorated column is removed and the element replaced. The replacement of a wooden lintel is more complicated as a greater number of bearing elements (such as vigas or beams) will require interim support, and professional assistance may be in order.

Pay careful attention to the nature of isolated detail — for it is frequently not uniform in historic vernacular structures — and a variety of woodworking details may actually be original. A good deal of the more subtle but interesting character of the Atencio house in Trampas (illustrated at the end of Chapter 2) lies in the fact that virtually every door and window is detailed slightly differently. It would be a mistake to violate the idiosynchratic character — and historic accuracy — of the building by regularlizing the varietally primitive Greek trim. Spontaneous inspiration is part of its charm!

Solution C:
Epoxy Resins

Modern advances in chemistry have created high-density epoxy resins which, injected into the wooden member, can bond deteriorated sections in non-structural, or occasionally even structural elements. Consult the manufacturer's specifications, and particularly if it is intended for a structural element, an experienced professional.

Solution D:
Taking Care Of Dry Rot

Moisture, darkness, and poor ventilation all contribute to a problem not untypical in old Southwestern woodwork: dry rot. Caused by the growth of a fungus under these conditions, the problem is also mentioned with reference to roof support structures, where it is most common, in Chapter 9. Symptoms are dry and crumbly areas of wood into which, say, a screwdriver can easily be pushed. Dry rot may also occur where there is adequate ventilation, as in exposed columns and exterior woodwork.

Anti-fungal liquids are available which,

painted in several heavy coats over deteriorated and adjacent areas, arrest the growth of the fungus. Good wood preservatives, like Woodlife (discussed in this chapter's Problem 1, Solution A), create an atmosphere most unsuitable for its reinstatement.

Of course, though the situation has been stabilized, this doesn't restore what is already virtually sawdust. Seriously rotted areas should be cut away to solid wood. Then replacement sections can be glued, screwed or dowelled into place. In severe cases, the entire wooden member may have to be replaced.

Solution E:
Protecting Columns From Seeping Water

Wood columns which rest directly on an exterior horizontal surface will soak up water through their exposed end-grain. This is a very typical problem with old (and poorly-designed new) buildings. Short of rebuilding the whole porch (covered in Problem 3), any effort to correct this condition will be helpful. If the column assembly can be lifted slightly — even ¼ to ½ inch — without dislodging the bottom anchor or disturbing the roof above, do so. Water-impervious materials, such as small flagstone shims, can be placed beneath.

If lifting the column is impractical or unsafe, at least apply a good amount of wood preservative and fill the entire base cavity with silicone: a useful, if temporary, form of therapy. In appropriate styles, such as Territorial, a small, well-caulked wood shoe or *plinth* (standard in the Classical formal vocabulary, originally for the same water-deterring reasons), may be built. Do not create a concrete ring, as this will only pool water where it is most detrimental. A variety of solutions are illustrated in the accompanying drawing.

Solution F:
Repair & Replacement Of Rotted Canales

Flat-roofed buildings with parapet walls need good canales, or water spouts, to channel water away from the roof and walls. These must be well flashed where they pass through parapets, as water trapped here will seep into the walls and roof. Because they endure far more water than other wooden components, they are most prone to rot.

Various styles have different canal details, and these should be preserved or restored in rehabilitation. For example, don't put Spanish Colonial or Pueblo Revival scrolled pieces on a Territorial building, unless they represent a significant and known feature of its historic evolution. Likewise, stone and hollowed-log canales have been used historically in the Indian pueblos, and they are too distinctive to consider replacement with other modern materials (as has frequently been done with short sections of sheet metal, eave gutter, flattened tin cans, or anything else that might have been handy). While this may — remotely — be rationalized as a natural extension of an evolving vernacular building tradition, it certainly does little for the historic integrity of the architecture.

If an existing canal can be repaired, it should be. If replacement of part or the whole element is necessary, replicate or restore to the original design. Correct and substantial flashing is of the utmost importance: metal is the best solution. Particularly in poorly-

PROTECTING COLUMNS FROM SEEPING WATER
This is a frequent problem with structures everywhere, including those of the historic Southwest, where generally dry conditions may have encouraged early builders toward fast and easy — but short-lived — solutions to column seating.

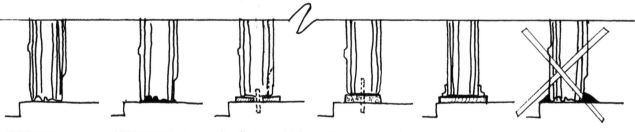

PROBLEM:
Columns rot if bottom end-grain exposed to water.

SOLUTIONS:
Silicone caulk; be as thorough as possible. Temporary but easily done.

Small stone chinking. Do not disturb pinning. Replace missing pieces of wood column.

New concrete shoe. Consider new pinning.

Territorial wood shoe. Short lifespan but convenient; toe-nail in place.

DO NOT make a 'protective' crater. It will only trap water.

Always rehabilitate historic elements wherever feasible; and only replace them when absolutely necessary. Nails, glue, clamps and wood preservative are all this broken canal needs.

insulated roofs, snow melted by heat loss from the building becomes water, which then freezes when no longer heated — as it passes through the wall, at the canal. This causes considerable duress to even the best sealing techniques — as water seeps in, freezes and expands, then melts out — leaving a forever-widening gap.

In some of the more deluxe constructions of the 20th century Revivals, electric resistance heaters were actually installed at canales to keep water in its liquid state until off the roof. (Like the strange-but-true heated driveway of the post-War Midwestern ranch house, this seems a bit extravagant in today's energy economy.) Given an inherently problematic condition, good insulation and serious flashing seem like the best solutions.

Comments and diagrams on how to manage water at the foot of the canal drop are included in the preceding Chapter 9 on roofs. Also discussed there is the deterioration and replacement of cantilevered exterior vigas.

Problem 3:
Structural Sagging Or (Even) Separation Of A Porch From The Building

Structural sagging of a porch is usually caused by differential soil bearing of the building and its attachments, inadequate foundations under one or both of the parts, or the erosive effects of water on the site.

Solution A:
Repair

Occasionally (if the problem is not too serious) a sagging porch can be lifted back into place with the assistance of screw-type building jacks, and the foundation repaired to hold it in place. This is usually not very difficult, though it looks rather elaborate while in process. Make sure the junction of the porch roof

and building wall is correctly repaired (which means, among other things, correctly flashed and attached), and that the underlying causes of the problem have been analyzed and addressed, such as gradual site erosion.

Solution B:
Rebuilding

If a sagging problem is beyond the scope of repair, then the entire porch structure may have to be removed and built again. This is a major undertaking, but not beyond the skills of most do-it-yourself carpenters. Record the historic porch in its existing condition first — with photographs and dimensioned drawings, numbering or otherwise coding the pieces. Dismantle it carefully and store the components, replicating any that might be missing or beyond reclamation at this time. Reassemble it again after new footings have been laid to the required depth, on firm bearing.

If the structure is too far gone to consider reassembly, it can be replicated in its entirety; but this may be more expensive than a well-considered rehabilitation. Try to reuse any old pieces, as they are better kept with the original building than discarded or sold off as architectural antiques. Even if only one column or one balluster can be salvaged, do so. These are historic artifacts and deserve to be treated as such. Also, they will help to establish what an accurate job was done in the restoration!

Solution C:
Reconstruction

Old photographs and other documentation sometimes indicate that porches or other historic architectural features may now be missing altogether. It may be desirable to reconstruct these, particularly if a porch existed on the west for shade, or if the covered space would otherwise serve the utility of the building. Almost certainly, reconstruction is likely to enhance the architectural value of the building.

Unless a serious restoration is planned, think twice about the reconstruction of a deep south-facing porch, as it will shade the wall from useful winter sun and make for rather dark rooms within. As outlined in Appendix A

REPAIRING OR REPLACING A CANAL
Often, flat-roof rain spouts, or canales, can be repaired;
but sometimes they must simply be replaced, for they
are among the wooden elements most prone to rot in
historic Southwestern buildings. This section illus-
trates the components, adapted to modern materials
and roofing techniques.

Chapter 9, 'Roofs,' also illustrates some of the tradi-
tional approaches to canal construction in the Indian
pueblos: the simple, but practical, antecedents to con-
temporary Revival styles.

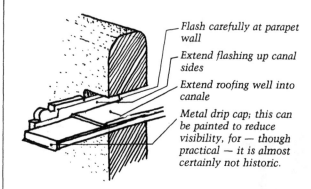

Flash carefully at parapet wall

Extend flashing up canal sides

Extend roofing well into canale

Metal drip cap; this can be painted to reduce visibility, for — though practical — it is almost certainly not historic.

on documenting the history of the building, be certain of the period to which the restoration belongs, for most of the older buildings in the Southwest have evolved over time.

ENERGY AND PORCHES IN SOUTHWESTERN ARCHITECTURE

In regional architecture of the Southwest, climate-adaptive qualities generally have more to do with the overall building envelope than with the particular nature of the architectural detail. And as historical review suggests, the same basic (frequently adobe) envelope has been rendered in any number of styles with changing times and popular tastes.

The number and placement of openings, and the location of porches bear, however, on the overall thermal performance of the building. By and large — though certainly not without exception — vernacular builders used some wisdom in these considerations, as shown in the consistent formula for massing in the Penasco Valley, as described in Chapter 5. If entry was from the north, these houses often had a covered porch running the length of the building. This provided a good place to store firewood and a degree of windbreak, reducing heat losses of the north wall. Shallow south porches provided a sheltered outdoor space, also reducing heat loss on the wall; and if shallow or high enough, admitted winter solar radiation to the surface, while shading in the summer.

As a general consideration, a porch located on the west side of an historic (or modern) building is the most effective in shading the wall from the extreme heat of summer afternoons. Where vigas project from the wall, they can be, and sometimes historically have been, used to support lightweight shading material during the summer, such as brush or reed mats. These must be secured in place against the ravages of wind and are best seasonal, to be removed during the winter.

CONSERVATION CONSIDERATIONS WITH PORCHES AND WOODWORK

Energy conservation is probably not a major factor in the preservation of historic woodwork and porches in the Southwest. Unlike the basic building envelope, they have more to do with architectural style. But, bear in mind the potential benefits of intelligent placement and proportion in their reconstruction or addition. A deep south portal would shade the wall and adjacent rooms from the warming winter sun, while a west orientation for a porch would provide valuable shading on hot summer afternoons. The woodwork attendant with doors and windows contributes importantly to historic character, and is considered in the following Chapter 11.

One consideration of conservation related to exterior woodwork in the arid Southwest might be the utilization of rainwater, collected from a pitched (or flat) roof. The addition of rain gutters is presented in the preceding Chapter 9 on roofs.

CHAPTER 11

DOORS & WINDOWS

A substantial variety of the Southwest's historic buildings are built with generally the same envelope: thick adobe or stone walls, and log or lumber roofs, flat or pitched. Doors and windows — collectively known as fenestration — are often the most distinguishing single factor in the building's character and style. They create key compositional counterpoint to the broad, continuous wall surfaces.

For the prehistoric Indians of the Southwest, doors and windows consisted primarily of small openings in wall and ceiling, covered seasonally by hides, mats or textiles. Spanish conquerors brought metal tools, and slowly — very slowly — adzed wood was employed in pintled (dowel-hinged into the frame at top and bottom) door and window shutters. Selenite (a transluscent mineral like mica) and oiled rawhide were still the only 'glass.' Metal hardware brought overland from Mexico was very scarce. It was popularized only slowly during the 17th through the 19th centuries, as local forges were established. Because little fenestration existed during or survives from the pre-Columbian and Spanish Colonial eras, very old doors and windows should certainly be considered of special merit in preservation.

The Santa Fe Trail opened access to trade with the Midwest in 1823. By 1838, glass found one of its earliest uses on the Customs House in Santa Fe; as trade became more routine; panes of glass became larger. By 1850, sawmills and brick kilns had been established and the American Greek Revival was introduced in the Southwest, in the regional idiom of the Territorial style. Window sash, doors, and Greek moldings were at first created with hand planes; on earlier buildings they frequently demonstrate considerable liberties in

Zaguan doors, with inset pedestrian passage, as they would have appeared in the context of a Spanish Colonial hacienda. Rancho de las Golondrinas, La Cienega, New Mexico.

The Anasazi, prehistoric Master-builders of the South-west, made doorways in a limited variety of configurations. The most distinctive is the "T-doorway," of which this is one of the largest examples from Pueblo Bonito at Chaco Canyon.

The functional — or symbolic — significance of the shape, which survived into the late 19th century, is not known, though a number of ideas have been advanced by archaeologists. In any case, provisions for covering these doors during the winter seem to have been simple — consisting of hides or textiles. Despite apparent limitations in climate control, they must have contributed significantly to the visual character of prehistoric architecture.

their rustic rendition of the classical types. By the mid 1860s, at the conclusion of the Civil War, these woodwork details began to assume more sophisticated forms.

With the arrival of the railroad in the early 1880s, contemporary Southwestern architecture looked — for a few decades at least — rather like the rest of the country, only retarded by the effects of time and space. For about 30 years, a broad-based eclecticism held the fort of regional tastes. Standard architectural fittings of every manner were used in new construction, and installed on existing buildings, though high cost kept their use in most but the fanciest buildings quite limited.

Revival-style architecture everywhere often exhibits particular liberties over the historic models of door and window treatment. This is certainly the case in the Southwest. Territorial Revival generally elaborates both degree of detail and scale and proportion beyond actual period antecedents; Pueblo Revival conveniently supposes the very fact of doors and windows as we know them, for they barely existed in original period construction. (Few 20th century people want to enter their houses through a hatch in the roof, it seems.) This Revival-style artistic license of superimposition continues to this day, and is seen in its most rational — if extreme — form in the contemporary puebloid solar adobe: combining unprecedented expanses of glass with a massing rooted in regional tradition.

As stated earlier, door and window fenestration is absolutely crucial to the character of most historic buildings. This can be especially true in this region, for sometimes there isn't much else going on architecturally. Proportion, composition in elevation, detail, and trim are all essential to the overall scheme. Basic maintenance and preservation is important, but not difficult. Conservation retrofits,

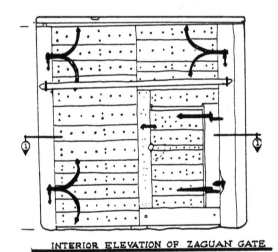

INTERIOR ELEVATION OF ZAGUAN GATE

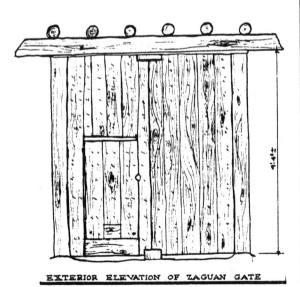

EXTERIOR ELEVATION OF ZAGUAN GATE

Zaguan gates from the Horace Long house, Ranchos de Taos. One of the finest surviving examples of its type, this door was the main entrance to the Spanish Colonial zaguan and plazuela. Double doors were opened to admit wagons, and the inset door was for routine pedestrian entry. Note hand-forged iron hinges (Fort Burgwin Research Center, Southern Methodist University)

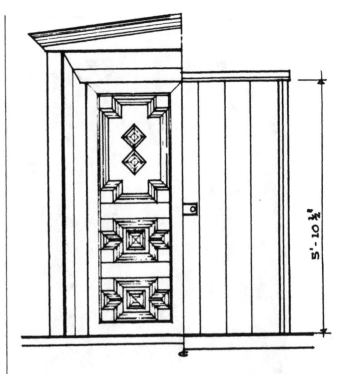

such as storm windows, need not detract from the historic appearance, if done properly.

PRESERVATION OF HISTORIC DOORS & WINDOWS

Like other areas of the country, woodwork of all kinds — especially that of doors and windows — is subject to deterioration over time. The relatively light framing and frequent movement of doors and windows contributes to their accelerated demise. In the Southwest, where fenestration is such a critical factor — often *the* critical factor — of a building's period character, its conscientious preservation is especially important. Though repair and replacement is a fairly routine matter, it is alarming to see, for example, the number of off-the-shelf aluminum units which

have taken the place of good, interesting and valuable historic elements in expedient or even ruthless renovation.

In terms of conservation, 27% of all heat loss in the average New Mexico home is through doors and windows — perhaps higher for adobe buildings, which have more thermally-stable walls. Next to basic weatherstripping and roof insulation, this may be the best place to concentrate effort in conservation. Double glazing can cut heat loss at windows in half. Done properly, it is also one of the places least likely to affect the historic appearance of the building.

Most of this region's historic doors and windows are not unlike those in other parts of the country; it is their combination with indigenous building envelopes (i.e., adobe) which lend them distinction. Neither preservation nor conservation problems and solutions are unique to this region; therefore, they are summarized only briefly here. More extensive information in both areas is included in other specific references, noted in the Bibliography.

No matter what the effort (or expense, for, hopefully, there will always be programs or financial incentives for proper preservation), this kind of historic detailing can never be replaced. Good preservation techniques assure that the best of historic architectural features endure — to the benefit of building owners, the neighborhood, and future generations alike.

Problem 2:
Serious Deterioration

Solution:
Replacement

Even the loosest-fitting door or window sash can usually be reassembled to sound condition if the wood is still solid. But if the wood itself is too far gone to consider rehabilitation, the entire element can be replaced. If cheap non-historic elements are tired and worn — and they were inclined to quick demise — replace them with more characteristic, or better yet, accurate historic elements. Particularly after the 1880s, dimensions are generally more standardized so it may be possible to find used doors or window sashes of the correct size.

Divided-lite steel industrial window sash is frequently seen in Revival Style buildings of the 1920s to 40s. Though its energy efficiency is low, worse things have been visited upon regional architecture; and it does have a certain period design integrity. Storm windows are considered in the following pages.

In no case resort to the type of rude modifications shown for this Italianate window (at right): the stock aluminum sliding window. Doors of the same genre are just as bad. Though the temptation may exist — because these seem inexpensive — don't indulge it. These windows have hidden problems aside from their devastating impact on the architecture. They are frequently a security problem, as they can easily be removed from the outside, and their metal frames lose heat far faster than wood. As stated earlier, because doors and windows form such key elements in the region's characteristically spare architectural schemes, correct historic features are especially important to preserve, or if necessary, replace with sensible reproductions.

ENERGY & HISTORY
IN REGIONAL FENESTRATION

Design for human comfort is apparent in

Problem 1:
Minor Wear-And-Tear

Solution:
Preservation & Basic Repair

Wood treated well will last almost forever in the Southwest. Good preservatives and solutions to splintering and dry rot are discussed in Chapter 10, Porches and Woodwork. If the whole unit is loose because of old dried wood and loose joints, rebuilding it from the same components is no great task, and is covered fairly extensively in other sources on historic preservation (consult Bibliography).

Even a double-hung window which is a bother because it has lost its counter-weight is fairly easy to repair though such elegant technical developments are fairly rare in earlier historic buildings in the Southwest. If the owner doesn't care to go to the trouble, someone in the neighborhood probably can. The cost of good rehabilitation is generally lower than the cost of replacement, in the long run at least. Why pay for a substitute unit from a fabricator in Cleveland (who has never even seen the building, and could care less) when the handyman down the street can rebuild it with some craftsman's pride, while keeping the money in the local economy?

the placement of doors and windows in much of the Southwest's historic Indian and Spanish architecture. At the same time, if they were covered at all, it certainly wasn't very tightly. Perhaps good orientation was devised to compensate for unremitting infiltration.

Territorial innovations — including glass windows — upgraded the standards of human comfort markedly; but it seems there is increasingly less evidence of preferential orientation. Natural lighting, weathersealing and ventilation are improved; intrinsic energy optimization is not. Over time, it would appear that regional builders frequently lost a sensitivity to the site and climate, and their explicit problems and potentials, particularly with regard to massing and orientation. (Maybe this is because more buildings were designed by architects, and fewer by the people who had to use them. More easily obtainable energy certainly made a difference in attitude.) Of course, there are notable exceptions and a number of them are illustrated in Part I.

In the rehabilitation of historic buildings, the combined wisdom of early folk-builders and modern energy technology can work toegether to make structures more efficient than they originally were, as suggested in the following problems and solutions.

Problem 3:
Excessive Heat Loss At Doors & Windows

According to data provided by the Public Service Company of New Mexico, for the average home in the state, 27% of heat loss occurs at doors and windows, with an additional 17% here due to infiltration. Both of these are easy to address. Properly done, they are unlikely to infuence the historic character of the building, and should be given a high priority in any renovation or conservation retrofitting plans.

Solution A:
Weathersealing

A large percentage of heat loss is often due to infiltration (air leaking out or in) around doors and windows. This can be dramatically reduced by caulking cracks between stationary elements (such as the doorstop and jamb) and weatherstripping around moving parts) such as between the door and doorstop in the frame). A variety of types of weatherstripping can be found, including spring metal, felt, foam rubber, and vinyl; choice will depend on the specific demands of the situation. One type alone will seldom handle all areas in a building. Fiber brushes and a variety of gasket types are available as threshold sweeps for doors, and will prevent some serious drafts.

An illustration from Rehab Right, *a very good book dealing with preservation among historic buildings in Oakland, California. A typical Bay-area Italianate window is shown, with the detrimental impact of inappropriate window revisions.*

In a sense, though historic Southwestern architecture is simpler in detail, such crass retrofits would prove even more devastating, as each feature in the nominal scheme is so crucial. (City of Oakland, California, Planning Department, Rehab Right)

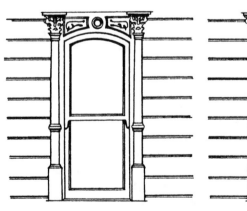

ORIGINAL DOUBLE-HUNG WINDOW (ITALIANATE).
DO LEAVE IT INTACT OR REPAIR OR REPLACE IN-KIND. WINDOWS ARE A KEY INTEGRAL PART OF THE ARCHITECTURE.

OPENING BLOCKED DOWN TO ACCEPT STOCK ALUMINUM FRAME,
DON'T DO THIS. IT LOOKS MAKESHIFT AND MARS THE PROPORTIONS AND APPEARANCE OF THE HOUSE.

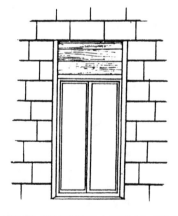

ORNAMENTATION REMOVED TO PUT ON ASBESTOS SHINGLES. NEVER DO THIS. TOTAL LOSS OF VISUAL INTEREST RESULTS.

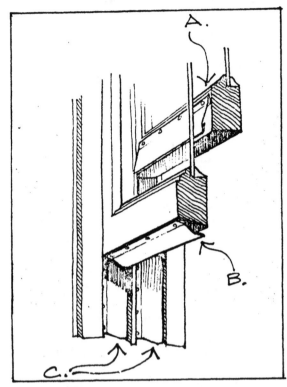

Several grades of weatherstripping materials are available: cheaper versions may deteriorate within a few years, or even less; higher quality materials will last much longer. When one considers the time and bother of installing either type, the more durable ones are probably a better choice.

Everyone agrees that all living and work spaces need some continuous ventilation. But in an old building, even the best weather-sealing won't stop infiltration entirely, so one needn't be unduly concerned with the prospect of suffocation. Beyond basic use patterns, weatherstripping and caulking are the cheapest, easiest and least obtrusive solutions to energy conservation, so do it first!

Solution B:
Storm Windows & Doors & Double Glazing

Heat loss at windows can be cut in half by double glazing, further still by triple glazing on unfavorable (usually north) orientations. This can be accomplished by including factory-sealed double glazed units in major renovation or by the addition of properly-sized storm windows. Storm doors may also be used to cut heat loss, but are sometimes more difficult to detail for compatibility with historic features. It is often better to concentrate effort at doors on careful weathersealing against infiltration.

Traditional storm windows, with or without seasonally interchangeable screens, may be installed without adverse visual impact, if they are well-proportioned. Even if original units can't be found today, old mounting hardware sometimes reveals their historic presence. Used replacement units of compatible dimension can sometimes be found. If damaged, glass or wire screening is easily replaced.

Likewise, new convertible units (with sliding and stationary glass and screen) may be used, but they must be correctly dimensioned, and, if possible, set back from the surface of the exterior frame and painted to minimalize their visual presence. Annodized finishes, like bronze and black, are now available, and usually superior to the shiny aluminum of earlier models.

Techniques for building simple wood frames with stretched clear vinyl — as a less expensive alternative — are discussed in home improvement and conservation books. Do not use frosted or translucent polyethylene films, as they obscure views out and prevent a clear view of the window framing muntins, important proportional features.

Solution C:
Insulating Shutters, Blinds Or Drapes

Particularly on north exposures, insulating shutters, blinds or drapes will help cut night heat-loss at windows. Incorporated into the interior of the window reveal, these may range from the simplest foam panels with magnetic clips (stowed away when not in use), to carefully fitted and detailed folding shutter assemblies. Even simple roll-down shades or adjustable blinds will help, and some of them come with special energy-efficient materials and finishes.

Whatever is done, it should be as unob-

A. Use replica of glazing pattern or (for door) double-glaze glass areas only. Avoid artificial wood or plastic insert muntins.
B. Unit proportioned to match primary structure.
C. A single large light of glass or acrylic glazing.
D. DO NOT use mismatched elements which ignore the historic patterns.
E. DO NOT use standard off-the-shelf units, especially those with 'industrial-Baroque' details.

trusive — or architecturally integrated — as possible: sensitive to the detail and proportion of the historic fenestration. Avoid heavy-handed drapery treatments, with swags and valances (unless particularly suited, for example, to Victorian window conditions and period furnishings). They more often obscure — rather than enhance — architectural lines.

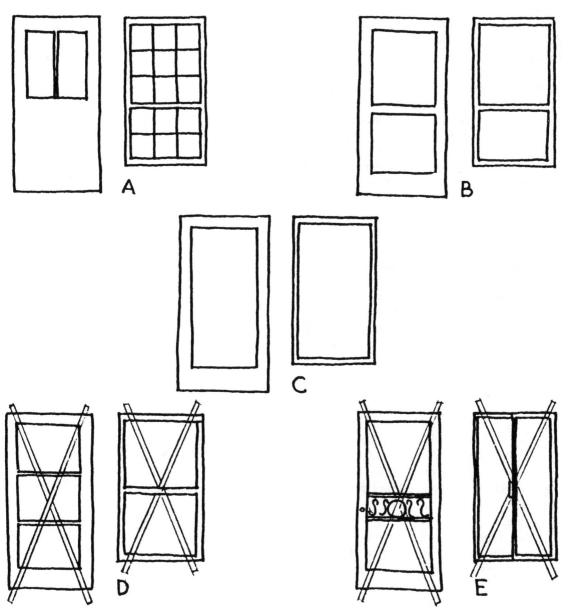

137

PART III:
ENERGY &
THE OLD BUILDING:

INTRODUCTION:
AGING GRACEFULLY THROUGH PRESERVATION & ADAPTATION

The American Southwest is among the global forefront in the development and implementation of solar heating technology. (After all, the Anasazi seem to have understood something about it 1,000 years ago!) As a result of solar's climatic appropriateness and broad public acceptance, an increasing number of buildings in the region are being retrofitted (changed with the addition of solar features). This is particularly evident in the temperate zones of the Colorado Plateau and the northern Rio Grande: with 6000 to 7500 degree days, not exactly the saguaro-cactus desert in which many people envision the entire Southwest! Many of these structures are either historic (at least 50 years old), or part of officially designated or unofficially perceived historic districts.

Too frequently, solar retrofitting tends to compromise the integrity of historic buildings (not unlike an 80-year-old woman donning a mini-skirt). But this need not be the case. The concluding part of this book suggests how preservation and conservation can work together in the maintenance and rehabilitation of historic regional buildings. This requires some information, thought, and planning.

Every building is different, both in its architectural particulars and in its contribution to the character of its neighborhood. A charming, if somewhat ordinary building — the Cecelia Cordova house in Santa Fe — is the subject of a sample case study, presented in Chapter 13. Many of the issues involved in its preservation, and possible solar adaptation are typical for a wide range of buildings in the Southwest.

But again, each building needs to be assessed for its own individual qualities: its historic style and architectural merits, the needs and resources of the owners or occupants, and its intrinsic potentials for adaptation. As with people, buildings aging gracefully usually demand some adaptation, and always benefit from a degree of artfulness.

CHAPTER 12

REHABILITATION & ADDITIONS

This window is in bad shape. But it is not beyond rehabilitation! While the sash may want to be replaced with double-glazing, do not do so at the expense of removing the divided-lite pattern.

The casing — and the carpenter-scrolled pediment in particular — is among the rich variety which lends tremendous historic character to the town of Chimayo, New Mexico. (See Chapter 2.)

This and the following chapter show how projects should be carefully planned — whether they are to be done in one grand gesture, or incrementally, as necessity demands, and time and resources allow. Professional consultation may be especially helpful in the planning phase, even if most of the work will be done by the owner. A coherent strategy toward style is the first step. Good planning will help avoid many pitfalls, saving both time and money. A careful examination of costs and benefits of specific jobs will help in knowing what to do first and what to save until later. Priorities should be set. Particularly if a certain job is rather expensive, how can it do more than one thing? Solve more than one problem? Contribute to the finished result, and not have to be redone or revised later?

Lifestyles have changed over the years, and many historic buildings, particularly those built in the Southwest before 1880, have floor plans which are problematic in adapting to contemporary use patterns. The classic situation is a structure built in a single file of rooms, one deep. The overall form may be a straight line, an L, T, U, or completely enclosed placita, but the problem remains the same: having to go through each room to get to the next, or going outside. Especially in the placement of bedrooms (which are generally more private today than on the frontier) this is a characteristic problem. Older houses here, which have been modified over the years, are notorious for oddities such as having to go through the bathroom to get to the kitchen or bedroom. The problem remains the same in adaptive use, such as the conversion of an old house into offices. Maybe charming, but the novelty wears thin with the inconvenience.

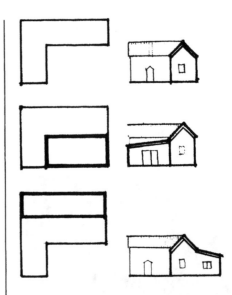

Typical 18th and 19th century adobe house, one room deep, with late 19th century pitched roof.

Addition made to the interior of the L-shape, facilitating circulation but eliminating protected outdoor space, and compromising nice architectural lines (and probably enveloping good period doors and windows as well).

Addition made on the outside of the long axis of the L. Frequently this is the north, colder side of the building.

In modern times, the most typical solution has been to add a row of rooms along one side of the existing structure. This helps zone circulation and private space, but usually compromises the beauty and clarity of the original, attenuated massing; and often as not, it eats up the defined and protected outdoor space in the process. Frequently, these additions are made with materials such as uninsulated cement block and aluminum frame windows — neither as energy efficient nor as attractive as earlier construction. Just the same, ways must be found to make old buildings work today, so additions are inevitable. Facing this choice, the question is how to do it and preserve the historic fiber and character of the existing structure.

PHILOSOPHY OF STYLE

There are two basic philosophies with regard to style in making additions to historic buildings. The first is that additions should fit in, and be compatible and similar; the second is that additions should be clearly new and distinguished from older sections. A 1969 addition to the Cordova house (explored in the following case study) is a reasonably good example of the first type, as it continues the expected growth pattern within the traditional idiom. Mies van der Rohe's steel-and-glass addition to the Neoclassic Houston Museum of Fine Arts, and the industrial greenhouse-as-restaurant structure attached to the Romanesque Exeter Street Theater in Boston, are fine examples of the second, contrast mode; in both of these cases, precipitated by the necessity of additional space to house new functions — in the interest of keeping the original structures functionally or economically viable.

With additions, we are immediately in the arena of rehabilitation, and no longer looking at preservation, restoration, or stabilization, as defined in the Secretary of the Interior's Standards for Historic Preservation (see Appendix B). However, the more significant or rarer a structure, the more important it is not to compromise its historic character by intrusive additions, no matter what their form.

The Secretary of the Interior's Standards condone "keeping new additions and adjacent new construction to a minimum, making them compatible in scale, building materials and texture," as well as "using contemporary designs compatible with the character and mood of the building or the neighborhood." Among the list of "not recommended" rehabilitation practices are "designing new work which is incompatible with the other buildings in the neighborhood, in materials, size, scale and texture," and "imitating an earlier style or period of architecture in new additions, except in rare cases where a contemporary design would detract from the architectural unity of an ensemble or group. Especially avoid imitating an earlier style of architecture in new additions that have a completely contemporary function such as a drive-in bank or garage."

But what about a solar greenhouse addition? Solar retrofitting of older buildings in the Southwest has caught on — almost to the dimensions of a phenomenon — because people have seen proof that it works, and can provide most of the heat they need. The most popular solutions are greenhouses — which provide additional space for circulation, living and year-round gardening — and trombe walls — which fix a light-transmitting glazing directly over a mass wall, quickly and relatively inexpensively.

Both can be extremely disruptive to the

historic character of a building, but their practicality often wins out. Unfortunately, many additions of this nature are of the '2 x 4 and plastic' genre: cost effective but generally unsightly. There is virtually no historic antecedent in the Southwest for extensively-glazed structures (the Dorsey solar greenhouse is a notable exception; see Chapter 4), so it is hard to draw design cures from traditional applications. In light of the "completely contemporary function" of solar additions, it would appear that it might be best to make them "distinct from but compatible with" earlier construction — compromising the historic fabric as little as possible. In addition to basic preservation and conservation measures — which should always be done first — some general considerations regarding solar retrofitting of historic buildings are listed below:

• Consider which facades are 'public' and which are 'private.' Public facades face the street or road, or contribute to the visible character of the neighborhood. Private facades face away from the street, perhaps into the secluded space of the site. Either can be a principal facade, depending on its degree of architectural detail and finesse. The ideal condition for a solar retrofit would be a building with its *principal* facade on a public north side, and an undistinguished, private south facade; but this is only occasionally the case.

• Especially if public, principal facades are those best exposed to the sun — but would suffer from a modern addition — or if the building is of special historic merit, the insistent solar advocate might consider remote collectors, hidden from view — not attached to, but ducted into the building.

• Traditional materials, such as adobe and timber may be good choices for an addition, if they blend with what is already there. Historic porch details from the appropriate style, say Territorial, can usually be adapted to a glassed-in enclosure. The visual impact of large areas of glass can be minimized by the suggestion of a portal, with the glass set back from the surface, providing a visual foreground and some very helpful summer shading.

• If a solar addition is to go on a private, secondary facade, consider an honest and direct solution: a fabricated glass and wood or metal frame component greenhouse (this is probably what the Dorsey greenhouse was). This author's personal sentiment is that the type with curved glass at the eaves may be the most elegant choice here, as it is most clearly distinguished from the appearance of earlier work, and expresses — as does a mud plastered adobe wall with exposed wood lintels — qualities intrinsic to the materials and the technology of putting them together.

• Greenhouse additions are best built as independent structural units: if new construction abuts an historic wall — particularly if it is adobe — it is better to support it independently. Attaching directly to the wall may be difficult, and cause cracking with the additional load. It could also then be removed with relative ease in the event of later restoration.

• Landscape manipulation, such as planting and earth berms, can hide a great deal; but take care in their selection and placement, that they not shade the structure. Research may reveal historic landscape materials which aided in climate modification with simple, low-water consuming plants.

CHAPTER 13

A SAMPLE REHABILITATION WITH SOLAR OPTIONS

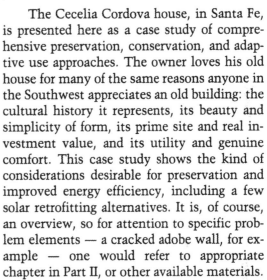

The Cordova house — like many historic buildings — has evolved over time; however, a consistent vocabulary of forms and materials ties all the parts together. While not exactly a candidate for the National Register of Historic Places, the house is 150 years old, and a rich chronicle of cultural change.

The Cecelia Cordova house, in Santa Fe, is presented here as a case study of comprehensive preservation, conservation, and adaptive use approaches. The owner loves his old house for many of the same reasons anyone in the Southwest appreciates an old building: the cultural history it represents, its beauty and simplicity of form, its prime site and real investment value, and its utility and genuine comfort. This case study shows the kind of considerations desirable for preservation and improved energy efficiency, including a few solar retrofitting alternatives. It is, of course, an overview, so for attention to specific problem elements — a cracked adobe wall, for example — one would refer to appropriate chapter in Part II, or other available materials.

The Cordova house was selected for this case study because it is rather typical of old adobe buildings in the Southwest. President Grant did not sleep here; it is not the biggest, oldest, or only example of its type; various additions have been made over the years, which have changed the original character of the architecture to a degree. But it is a good, comfortable building; and cheaper to rehabilitate than replace. Also, like many other buildings of native tradition, it has some very effective conservation features built-in.

This case study for the Cordova house is laid out according to the recommended documentation and planning process which any renovation project should follow, beginning with research on the history of the building. This is followed by an evaluation of integrated preservation and conservation approaches. Finally, there is a set of six alternative solar retrofitting strategies with notes on their functional intent, and impact on the

Plan and elevations of the Cecilia Cordova house in Santa Fe, as it appeared in 1980.

The south-facing, semi-enclosed plazuela of the Cordova house is an architecturally-created sun trap. The vaguely Queen Anne porch detail is modern, but looks old, for it is adapted from other rural 19th century houses in northern New Mexico's highlands.

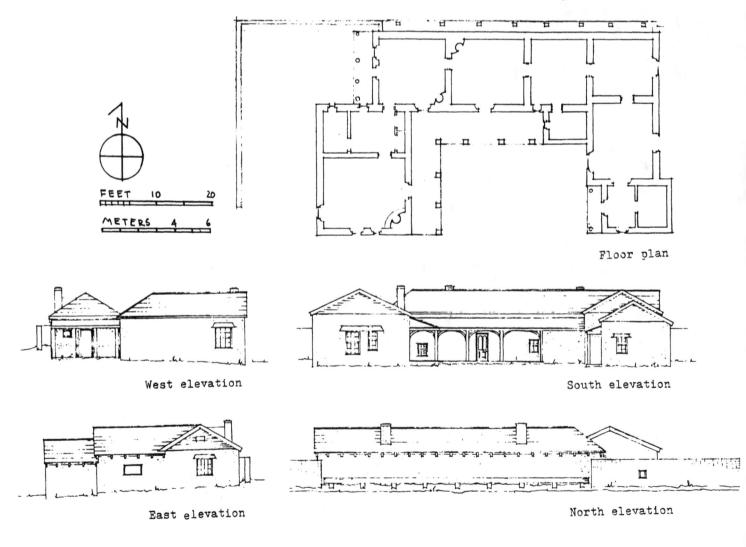

Floor plan

West elevation

South elevation

East elevation

North elevation

144

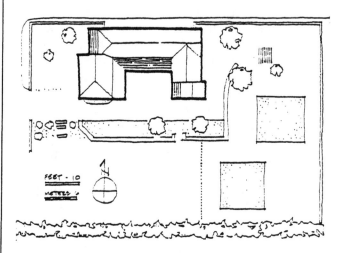

historic structure.

As the type of work discussed here would demand fairly substantial investments of time and money, such projects, at best, would address a greater range of problems than historic preservation or energy performance alone. The idea behind most of the solar retrofitting strategies is to solve more than one problem at once: like solar collection and airlock, and additional closet space; or solar collection and indoor gardening, and improvement in the circulation of the single-file plan. Again, these solar retrofitting proposals are probably not recommended for really significant or unique structures. But they represent realistic and relatively acceptable approaches to what today's pragmatic historic building owner may be likely to do anyway.

HISTORIC DOCUMENTATION

First, research was done to get a picture of the history of the building, and the evolution of the architecture. Sources which were helpful included old photographs, the verbal history of the owners' families and neighbors, and a property abstract. Scale plans and elevations of the existing house were drawn. Photographs were taken of the building as it exists today. (See Appendix A for suggestions.)

GROWTH OF THE HOUSE

ca. 1830: original three-room adobe farm house with flat earth roof.

ca. 1830: may be original, or added shortly thereafter.

1880-1903: pitched roof added over existing flat roof
1949: bathroom added at juncture of L

1969: new wings added to SW and SE corners, portales added on N and W of the plazuela and elsewhere

The original house was built around 1830, probably by M.N. Lovato, on the south-facing slopes of Cerro Gordo, in the broad canyon east of Santa Fe. Research suggests that the north and east wings of the five-room farmhouse were built about the same time, with a dry stoné foundation, 18'' adobe walls, and a flat earth woof. Windows (such as they were in 1830) and doors were confined to the south, east, and west sides, leaving a continuous, solid, and partially-buried north wall (similar to the Atencio house in Trampas. See Chapter 2), to abut the adjacent road. This provided good insulation and isolation from the noise and activity of the road. (Then it was foot traffic, horses and wagons; now it is mostly automobiles.)

A pitched roof was added before 1903, as revealed in an old photograph (future work on the roof may uncover the original pitched roofing material). More up-to-date Territorial doors, and additional windows, seem to have been added at this time. The house remained essentially unchanged until 1949, when a small bathroom was added at the junction of the north and east wings. In 1969 a new owner brought the need for substantial expansion, and a new wing was added to the southwest, together with a secondary entrance and storage room to the south of the existing east wing. The sequence of growth is illustrated in the accompanying series of plan diagrams.

This latest construction created a small, semi-enclosed plazuela, open on the south to a fine view of the irrigated fields, and exposed to the low winter sun. Summer shading was provided with a new, shallow portal along two sides of the plazuela. This portal was imaginatively designed — not in the expected Territorial — but with detached decorative arches (more typical of Queen Anne style, which enjoyed a limited popularity after 1880). This motif restated that of antique Victorian, arched glass-panel doors, probably installed as recycled components at this time. The entire wood construction of the portal, window sash, doors and trim was painted a surprising, though not unsightly, bright turquoise blue — a color of regional tradition.

The present owner has enclosed the property on the north and west with adobe walls, providing a windbreak, increasing visual privacy, and helping to isolate the increased activity of Cerro Gordo Road on the outside of the compound.

On the whole, each of these additions works well in its relationship to the original structure: maintaining a pattern of scale, texture, color and detailing compatible with earlier construction. As an assemblage of separate pieces constructed over a span of 150 years, the Cordova house seems to have succeeded in maintaining its native character, and evolving a sensible and regionally appropriate plan form. At the same time, it reflects the character and tastes of each of its owners. This is typical of the vernacular, folk-architectural tradition: with a set of unwritten rules, the idiom can adapt and grow within an established pattern; and similar massing, materials and details tie it all together. Not a museum piece of history, but a very real chronicle of culture.

Furthermore, the construction and overall configuration of the Cordova house make a good deal of sense in terms of energy efficiency: adobe walls and pitched roof providing for a high-mass building, with good insulation where it is most needed; siting on a warm south slope, with no openings on the bermed-in north wall; orientation of the plazuela, and most doors and windows, toward the south, thereby minimizing heat loss, while maximizing winter solar gain; and the addition of a portal along the perimeter of the plazuela for summer shading. Recent landscaping to the south promises some benefit in shading and evaporative cooling during the summer.

PRESERVATION AND CONSERVATION

The historic Cordova house is in reasonably good condition today; but as with any

CORDOVA HOUSE: PRESERVATION PLANNING
Problem

Erosion of mud plaster

Erosion at the base of the north wall, due to roof runoff and splash from cars passing on the road

Crack in the north adobe wall, below an old unused chimney

Excessive heat loss in the 1969 southwest wing addition

Excessive heat loss due to single glazing and serious air infiltration around doors and windows

Excessive heat loss in the southwest wing due to a large, undampered fireplace

Pitched roof sagging and warping due to inferior construction or inadequately dried wood, uneven settling, rotting or leaking

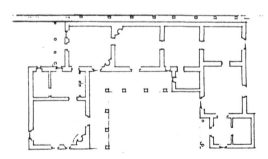

Preservation Approach	Conservation Approach	Savings, Cost & Payoff - 1980 estimate
— Replaster as necessary, with more frequent attention to areas of particular wear; match existing plaster for color, composition and texture	Keeping wall dry with a good plaster not only protects the adobe structure but improves thermal efficiency	Probably to be done every five years, taking about 6 man-days; essential to maintenance of adobe walls Very small materials cost
— Patch plaster in coved area; add roof gutters; consider a gravel-filled drainage ditch to divert ground water from seeping into the wall	Gutters added at all eaves of the 3000 square foot roof – with an average annual rainfall of 13.1 inches – would collect 26,000 gallons per year; it could be stored in cisterns or diverted to irrigation	26,000 gallons of water costs about $55 by 1980 Public Service Co. rates; 215 feet of gutter costs about $250.00 for materials; the owner can easily do the installation
— There is no interior fireplace so the brick chimney is not adequately supported, causing settling and possible leaking; remove the chimney, patch the roof well, and repair the adobe crack.	Benefit from improved seal against air infiltration	Bricks can be recycled on the site for construction or landscaping. A labor-intensive job with benefits in the structural future of the building
— This is due to the absence of an earth roof, as found in the older sections of the building, making for lower mass and less insulation	6-inch batt insulation can be installed in the attic space between ceiling and roof, improving thermal resistance from about R14 to R35	For the 650 square foot wing, materials would cost $170; labor is nominal
— Window sashes can be repaired or patched as necessary; storm windows and doors should be carefully selected for compatibility with historic elements	Weatherstrip all doors and windows, which saves on the average 5 - 10% of heating and cooling energy; storm windows and doors will save another 10 - 15%	Weatherstripping is one of the most cost-effective things to do; cost is nominal for materials which pay for themselves in 1 - 2 years; storm windows and doors, numbering 15, would cost between $1,000 and $1,500, depending on quality and detail; reasonable payoff time
— The 1969 fireplace is far larger than historic types — simply out of scale with the room and cramping furniture arrangement: consider cutting it down to a size similar to older fireplaces in the house	Make the aperture in the room smaller and install a damper and glass doors, or a recirculating system; bring air to feed the fire from unheated outside source	Fireplace efficiency jumps from 10% to 34% with these modifications
— A major reconstruction is not necessary at this time, but check all roll roofing material and flashing; check in attic for structural condition, or possible insect damage or leaks: if the roof is rebuilt or resurfaced, consider restoring to the original sheathing, probably metal	Roof insulation could be improved; if a resurfacing with metal is planned, the design could be modified for flush-glazed hot water collectors; and the 700 square foot south-facing section could be modified to an unglazed, flat plate collector, providing convective heat throughout much of the house, while remaining visually unobtrusive	Reconstruction of the roof would be expensive, costing perhaps $20,000 if done by a contractor, including the hot water and air collecting system; but it would improve the historic appearance of the house and yield benefits in thermal efficiency

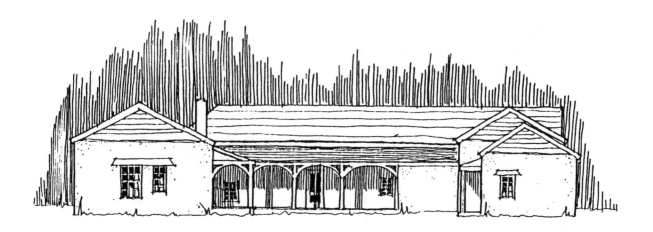

building, anywhere, there is some regular maintenance to be done, and ways in which energy efficiency can be further improved. Also, it is built of adobe — and this poses its own special series of challenges in preservation. In many cases these activities can be tied together in creative ways to solve several problems at once. The accompanying chart (pp. 146-7) lists some areas of attention, with notes on ways to address them for historic preservation and energy conservation. Specific how-to information for many of these operations can be found in Part II of this book. They are arranged roughly in order of increasing cost and complexity in this chart.

SOLAR RETROFITTING

The single-file plan of the Cordova house has its own intrinsic functional problems; and despite basic conservation measures, it will still cost plenty to heat. The owner is considering a solar retrofit, to solve both of these challenges. On the following pages, diagrams of several solar retrofitting strategies are presented. They address various concerns with different strategies, different costs, and different impacts on the architectural character of the building.

As a case study, these are intended to illustrate the potentials and consequences of various approaches. In the specific circumstances of this building — for the south facade is neither technically historic, nor is it publicly visible — each one achieves a certain goal, at a certain cost. The intention is to show that there are a variety of means to arrive at a solution. Some are better than others.

Every building — historic or not — is different, and requires a different treatment. But to its owner, an historic structure represents a very special asset, and merits careful consideration in preservation, addition or adaptive use. In the following Conclusion, the solid economics of demolition versus renovation are presented. Aside from the sentimental appeal of history, preservation proves to make a lot of sense.

CORDOVA HOUSE:
SOLAR RETROFITTING STRATEGIES

Solution

(A) Replace roll asphalt roofing with metal; south facing section can be framed as an unglazed flat-plate collector (700 sq. ft.); flush panels for water heating can be built in

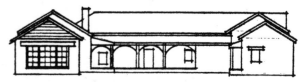

(B) Add solarium and vestibule / airlock in vernacular, form balancing southeast corner addition; large large direct-gain glass

(C) Glaze in portal, southfacing section; keep west open for wood storage, outdoor seating, garden access; must be ventilated; preserve access to plazuela

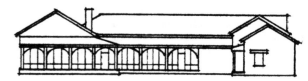

(D) Add continuation of glassed in portal to southwest corner, with airlock, in mode of existing Queen Anne style portal

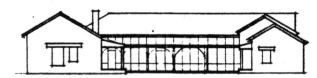

(E) Add glass 'gallery' 13 ft wide, connecting rooms; leave all existing architecture intact, encased in a transparent shell; existing portal roof becomes surface for hot water collectors, central to areas where water is used; floor area can be extra room or existing walkway with 200 square foot planting bed

(F) Add greenhouse off kitchen at northwest corner, facing south; convenient to kitchen; airlock option

Impact

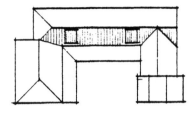

Minimum visual impact, does not help floor plan, raise main east/west axis roof pitch slightly (from 30 [4 in 12] to 37 [5 in 12])

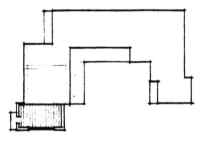

Keeping in the style of earlier additions; follow established pattern of growth; coordinate glazing with existing

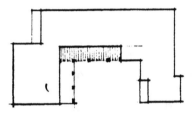

Some visual impact; diminish by setting glass back from colonnade; helps floor plan by connecting up to five rooms

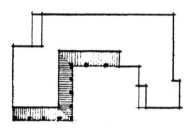

An artful, if slightly ambitious adaptation including non-historic but effective period motif; connects up to six rooms, providing superior, articulated circulation and airlock

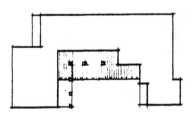

Major visual impact on private facade only; high solar efficiency; excellent solution for floor plan, connecting up six rooms; possibly the most effective and daring solution, and must be done with knowledge, sensitivity and design savvy

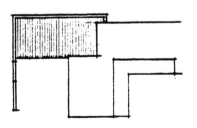

No impact on primary plazuela elevation; continues the idiom of attenuated wings in scale only — detailing and materials are frankly modern; moderate benefit to floor plan; very effective solar collection combined with ducting to house. Works well in combination with other options

149

CHAPTER 14

CONCLUSION:
ENERGY ECONOMICS
& THE GOOD SENSE OF
HISTORIC PRESERVATION

Scenes from the Southwest's Indian pueblos! No. A house and village in north Africa.

This book has focused on the history and preservation of Southwestern architecture with emphasis on buildings in New Mexico, and adobe structures in particular. Conservation issues have been a major theme: both the conservation of irreplacable 'soft' cultural resources, and the conservation of non-renewable 'hard' energy resources.

About the cultural worth of historic preservation, one who has read this far probably understands it already, and perhaps enough has been said. Though it is impossible to assign a concrete, monetary value to our built heritage, almost everyone senses it. Likewise, the human history of the Southwest — most visible in its buildings and built places — is an important reminder to indigenous cultures, and formidable drawing card in the region's continued attraction to bright, creative people and occasional tourists alike. Further cultural and economic assets.

About energy conservation and its relationship with historic buildings, it is possible to be somewhat more precise: rehabilitation of historic buildings — rather than demolition and new construction — generally costs less and uses less energy. There are other benefits as well.

With 6% of global population, the United States currently consumes 35% of world resources and energy. Construction and maintenance of buildings accounts for over 40% of all the energy consumed in this country. Yet savings of 25 to 35% of this energy are well within reach with current, simple conservation measures and technologies, and are potentially much higher with solar applications.

Rehabilitation and adaptive use of individual buildings and entire neighborhoods has

The Old Pension Building in Washington, D.C., now the new home of the National Museum of Building Arts. This wonderful brick structure seems distinguished among the white marble monuments of Washington and features several ingenious 19th century engineering solutions to climate control. These include clever ventilation slots below the pedimented windows, and a mammoth central light well, which facilitates both air movement and natural lighting. Built before advent of the totally controlled and energy-supported environment, many older buildings show the wisdom of built-in conservation features. (National Museum of the Building Arts)

developed a great momentum over the last 10 years, now accounting for about one-half of all building activity in the United States. More and more owners, investors, builders and design professionals are realizing the good sense of adaptive use and preservation. One of its additional advantages is that it tends to be labor-intensive, with larger amounts (say 75% rather than 50%) of the money staying in the local wage economy.

Rehabilitating existing buildings usually costs somewhat to substantially less than building new, and it uses less energy in the process. The following is excerpted from Baird Smith's *National Benefits of Rehabilitating Existing Buildings*, (U.S. Department of the Interior, Technical Preservation Services Division, October 1977):

An important recent study prepared for the Energy Research and Development Administration (ERDA) has investigated the amount of energy needed to build new buildings and the amount necessary to rehabilitate existing ones. The report is "Energy Use for Building Construction," by Richard G. Stein & Associates, Architects, and the Energy Research Group, Center for Advanced Computation, University of Illinois at Champaign-Urbana. The study surveyed all publicly advertised new construction and rehabilitation work for a base year (1967) in the United States to measure how many BTUs of energy is taken, on a square-foot basis, to extract, manufacture, deliver, and install all building materials, such as lumber, brick, and concrete. The researchers determined that it took 23% less energy to rehabilitate existing buildings. Specifically, it took an average of 49,900 BTUs/sq.ft. to rehabilitate as opposed to 65,200 BTUs/sq.ft. to build anew. This included all building types — residential, office, commercial and industrial... This lower energy consumption can be attributed to the fact that most of the structural systems and building materials were in place and reusable in the rehabilitation project.

...how much energy would be saved, in say 1982, if the rehabilitation movement increased from 32% to 39% of the construction market [which it more than has; ed.] with a resulting decrease in the amount of new construction[?]...The savings in energy would equal 30 million barrels of crude oil for the year. That is enough to provide all the energy needed for about 800,000 households for the year.

The inherent energy-efficiency of many historic buildings also makes a good case for their preservation. Research was done on a sample of 44 office buildings in New York City arranged according to period of construction. (Syska & Hennessy and the Tishman Research Corporation, for ERDA.) With utility cost (for

Dates	No. of Bldgs.	% of Bldgs.	% of Area	Energy Consumption Range (1000's of BTU's/sq.ft.)	Average Consumption (1000's of BTU's/sq. ft.)
Before 1900	3	6.8	1.1	83–115	95
1901–1919	8	18.2	12.8	76–135	105
1920–1940	18	40.9	28.3	68–223	109
1941–1962	12	27.3	36.2	66–198	126
1962–1970	3	6.8	21.6	78–163	115

This chart shows a selection of forty-four office buildings in New York City, examined over a period of five years, and their energy use by date of construction. Clearly the older buildings are more efficient. (Energy Conservation in Existing Office Buildings, Syska, Hennessy, Tishman Research Corporation; for ERDA, June 1977)

electricity, fuel oil, coal, etc.) evaluated over a five-year period, the oldest buildings (before 1900) proved to be the most efficient. This was attributed to several characteristics of design and construction — all absent from the later generations of sealed steel-and-glass boxes in the study:

WALL MASS   It has been determined that existing walls of large mass (thick brick or stone) have the advantage of "high thermal inertia." This inertia modifies the thermal resistance (R factor) of the wall by lengthening the time scale of heat transmission. For instance, a wall of high thermal inertia, subjected to solar radiation for an hour, will absorb the heat at its outside surface, but transfer it to the interior over a period as long as 6 hours. Conversely, a wall having the same R factor, but low thermal inertia, will transfer the heat in perhaps 2 hours.

RATIO OF GLASS-TO-WALL   Old buildings which have low ratio of glass-to-wall, less than 20%, will be better energy conservers than buildings with high glass-to-wall ratios because windows are a principal source of heat loss and gain.

OPERABLE WINDOWS   The fact that most old buildings have operable windows will result in measurable energy savings because the fresh outside air is readily available during mild months so that energy consuming heating and cooling systems will not have to be operated.

CAVITY WALL CONSTRUCTION   The presence of cavities in most masonry and wooden construction in old buildings provides a definite increase in the thermal resistance of the wall and increases the positive benefits of thermal inertia.
(Baird Smith, "National Benefits of Rehabilitating Existing Buildings," October 1977.)

Though the overall scale is certainly smaller, many of the Southwest's historic buildings exhibit the same qualities which make this urban sample work: high mass construction; a low ratio of glass-to-wall area; natural ventilation; and occasionally, cavity wall construction. Given the nature of the climate, and traditional adherence to these general principles in folk-construction, it is probable that historic buildings of the Southwest would fare even better than the urban sample. Indeed, monitoring of a typical regional building, at the Ghost Ranch Sundwellings Demonstration Center, indicated that this simple adobe building was already 28% efficient in passive solar operation. (Quentin Wilson, "Ghost Ranch Sundwelling Performance," *Southwest Bulletin: New Mexico Solar Energy Association*, June 1978.)

Thus, historic preservation seems to conserve not only the soft resources of a deep cultural heritage — a graphic touchstone with our place in time and space — but also, the hard energy resources which we find increasingly more scarce and expensive. Some of the inherent savings can be measured, some cannot.

It may be interesting to note that a crisis of overconsumption has brought us back to a new appreciation of the wisdom of indigenous construction, witnessed in the post-Modern theme of architectural regionalism. Historic architecture and town planning, here and elsewhere, often teach solid lessons in sensible response to climate and optimal use of limited resources.

Likewise, the materials of modern technology — such as larger areas of glass in contemporary passive solar design — can lend significantly to the energy performance, and continued usefulness, of older structures. Carefully considered, old and new need not be at odds. In fact, they can work well together, optimizing conservation while preserving the best of a rich architectural heritage.

**REHABILITATION
VERSUS
NEW CONSTRUCTION**

USUALLY COST LESS •

USES LESS ENERGY •

**KEEPS MORE MONEY IN •
THE LOCAL ECONOMY**

**PRESERVES UNIQUE •
CULTURAL RESOURCES**

APPENDIX A

HISTORIC BUILDINGS:
RESEARCH & DOCUMENTATION

Before beginning any work on an old building, the first thing to do is to find out as much as possible about its history. This research will be helpful in determining what is original, and the chronology of later changes or additions; where problem areas might lie; and identify period details that might be used in restoration. The process can be brief or quite elaborate. In any case, this detective work is often quite fascinating. The more you know of your building, the greater its value to you, both in knowledge and as a genuine investment in a high-priced antique.

First, look at the building carefully. What are its most prominent and identifying characteristics? To which historic period and style does it seem to belong? Look for distinguishing features, materials, and details. Furthermore, be sure to keep your eyes open for problem areas: try to determine whether or not a specific crack in an adobe wall, for example, is stable and unchanging, or recent and dramatic, and in need of immediate repair. A scale-drawing of the floor plan is an irreplaceable asset, and a good place to keep notes on the work to be done.

Do research on the building. The title, deed, or abstract will often contain some interesting information. A legal description of the property should be in your possession or in the official county record, and this will be helpful in further research. A chain of title (record of successive owners) can be established which might lead back, hopefully, to information on its original construction, and document subsequent development. Old maps will be especially helpful, and often show other features of the neighborhood and landscape.

A number of sources can be called upon in historic research. These include official state and city departments involved with historic preservation, local citizens' organizations, and museums. Museum, university and state libraries often have extensive photographic archives. City directories, county tax records (which are a good place to start, and often reflect the date of an addition with a change in tax assessment), and old newspapers (usually on microfilm) also provide facts and clues on the path of discovery.

Photograph the building, particularly if you are planning any modifications. Almost anyone with even the simplest camera can do this. Or ask a photographer friend or professional for assistance. Interior shots, in particular, often call for a wide-angle lens. Get pictures of the overall structure, landscaping, interiors, details and materials. Be sure to cover the entire building — a good, frontal photograph of each elevation is imperative. A slightly overcast day will minimize shadows and insure that key details don't get lost in the dark.

Old photographs can be among the most in-teresting and useful forms of historic documentation. Check the public record sources, but don't overlook old family albums, or pictures in the possession of neighboring property owners. Not infrequently, one will find photos with people as the apparent subjects, but in which the architecture appears. These can be quite revealing, and often helpful in dating particular features.

Talk to people: former owners, older neighbors, and family. They may be able to provide a lot of information in oral history, including construction dates, original builders, what different rooms were used for, earlier color schemes, and so on. Their memories and reflections of past days can be very charming, and lend unique insight and human history to the life of the building. "I remember the day your grandmother — she was only five or six back then — fell out of that old apple tree, and sprained her arm! There were 8 trees then, in two long rows, and the house was only three rooms..." Architectural and cultural history go hand-in-hand, and we cannot help but be enriched through their understanding.

APPENDIX B

OFFICIAL STANDARDS FOR PRESERVATION & REHABILITATION

The following guidelines are from a leaflet entitled "Historic Preservation Grants-in-Aid" prepared by the Office of Archaeology and Historic Preservation, Heritage Conservation and Recreation Service, U.S. Department of the Interior.

Acquisition and development work for registered properties must be completed in accordance with the Secretary of the Interior's Standards for Historic Preservation Projects. These standards have been developed for use by the Heritage Conservation and Recreation Service and the SHPOs and their staffs in planning, undertaking, and supervising grant-assisted projects for aquisition, protection, stabilization, preservation, rehabilitation, restoration, and reconstruction.

The following definitions are provided for treatments that may be undertaken on historic properties listed in the National register of Historic Places:

Acquisition is defined as the act or process of acquiring fee title or interest other than fee title of real property (including the acquisition of development rights or remainder interest).

Protection is defined as the act or process of applying measures designed to affect the physical condition of a property by defending or guarding it from deterioration, loss or attack, or to cover or shield the property from danger or injury. In the case of buildings and structures, such treat-ment is generally of a temporary nature and anticipates future historic preservation treatment; in the case of archaeological sites, the protective measure may be temporary or permanent.

Stabilization is defined as the act or process of applying measures designed to reestablish a weather-resistant enclosure and the structural stability of an unsafe or deteriorated property while maintaining the essential form as it exists at present.

Preservation is defined as the act or process of applying measures to sustain the existing form, integrity, and material of a building or structure, and the existing form and vegetative cover of a site. It may include initial stabilization work, where necessary, as well as ongoing maintenance of the historic building materials.

Rehabilitation is defined as the act or process of returning a property to a state of utility through repair or alteration which makes possible an efficient contemporary use while preserving those portions or features of the property that are significant to its historical, architectural, and cultural values.

Restoration is defined as the act or process of accurately recovering the form and details of a property and its setting as it appeared at a particular period of time by means of the removal of later work or by the replacement of missing earlier work.

Reconstruction is defined as the act or process of reproducing by new construction the exact form and detail of a vanishing building, structure, or object, or a part thereof, as it appeared at a specific period of time.

The following general standards apply to all treatments undertaken on historic properties listed in the National Register:

Every reasonable effort shall be made to provide a compatible use for a property that requires minimal alteration of the building structure, or site and its environment, or to use a property for its originally intended purpose.

The distinguishing original qualities or character of a building, structure, or site and its environment shall not be destroyed. The removal or alteration of any historic material or distinctive architectural features should be avoided when possible.

All buildings, structures, and sites shall be recognized as products of their own time. Alterations that have no historical basis and which seek to create an earlier appearance shall be discouraged.

Changes, which may have taken place in the course of time, are evidence of the history and development of a building, structure, or site and its environment. These changes may have acquired significance in their own right, and this significance shall be recognized and respected.

Distinctive stylistic features or examples of skilled craftsmanship, which characterize a building, structure, or site, shall be treated with sensitivity.

Deteriorated architectural features shall be repaired rather than replaced, wherever possible. In the event replacement is necessary, the new material should match the material being replaced in composition, design, color, texture, and other visual qualities. Repair or replacement of missing architectural features should be based on accurate duplications of features, substantiated by historical, physical, or pictorial evidence rather than on conjectural designs or the availability of different, architectural elements from other buildings or structures.

The surface cleaning of structures shall be undertaken with the gentlest means possible. Sandblasting and other cleaning methods that will damage the historic building material shall not be undertaken.

Every reasonable effort shall be made to protect and preserve archaeological resources affected by, or adjacent to any acquisition, protection, stabilization, preservation, rehabilitation, restoration, or reconstruction project.

CRITERIA FOR ALTERATIONS TO REGISTERED HISTORIC SITES

Excerpted from: New Mexico State Planning Office: The Historic Preservation Program for New Mexico; Santa Fe, 1973; Volume I: The Historical Background; pp. 103-104.

Registered historic sites should be removed from the State and National Registers when, in the opinion of the Cultural Properties Review Committee, the sites have been changed to the extent that their historic and architectural integrity has been impaired and register status is no longer valid. For many of the unique sites in New Mexico no generalized criteria are applicable. Each case must be judged upon the basis of specific criteria applicable only to that specific site. In the interest of justice, promptness and consistency, however, general criteria may be derived which are applicable to most of the registered sites in New Mexico.

Any construction other than routine maintenance and repair applied to an historic building decreases the building's genuineness and ideally should be avoided. Unfortunately, conditions of excellent maintenance throughout many years are rarely found; most historic structures have been neglected for so long that their preservation is dependent upon some degree of repair, stabilization, or even major restoration. Some buildings have been preserved in their original condition as museums and such use has been an excellent means of insuring their long range preservation. However, adaptation to new uses is one of the most effective methods of preserving many historic buildings, but such adaptation typically involves some new construction. From minimal stabilization and repair to extensive rehabilitation and restoration, or in rare cases relocation or rebuilding, new construction of some kind is needed in most sites which have been placed on the New Mexico State Register of Cultural Properties or the National Register of Historic Places. Adaptive use of historic buildings, properly conceived and executed, can be a most valuable tool for preservation. It must be

recognized, however, that the extent and quality of such work if not properly conceived can diminish the integrity of a site to the degree that the State or National Register status should be revoked. Therefore, it is of great importance to develop criteria for changes in historic buildings in order that damage can be avoided and the effect of the new work upon the integrity of a registered site can be consistently and quickly evaluated.

Only one criterion is clearly applicable to registered sites of all kinds. All changes must be thoroughly recorded and the documentation must be placed in the most reasonable repository where it is always available to researchers. One copy should be placed in the archives of the State of New Mexico Records Center and another should be filed in the most appropriate institution nearest the site, such as a public library and the library of a college or university. A copy of this data should also be sent to the Cultural Properties Review Committee wherever possible, such documentation should be displayed at or within the historic building or site so that any recent work is clearly explained to the interested visitor. The owners of registered sites who are concerned with preserving the registered status should submit complete plans and details of any proposed changes to the Cultural Properties Review Committee for its evaluation before such changes are begun.

Comprehensive criteria applicable to changes in all historic sites have been subjected to two categorizations, based upon the nature and the degree of the value which the site possesses.

A comparison between the 17th century mission of Abo and the Rafael Borrego house in Santa Fe demonstrates the need for the first categorization, based upon the kind of value which the site has. Although Abo has visual quality and recreational potential, its predominant values are scientific and educational. No responsible preservationist would consider seriously any new work at this site other than essential and clearly defined stabilization, as well as additional excavation and research. The Borrego house, however, is one of many registered Territorial period houses in New Mexico. It is not only capable of sheltering an economically productive function, in this case a restaurant, but such adaptation to a new use is probably the most reasonable way of assuring the preservation of the house. The quality of change which is appropriate to the adaptation of the Borrego house to a new use would destroy the primary values of the Abo site. Different criteria are clearly required for the two sites because they have values which fall into different categories

A comparison between the Church of San Jose de Gracia at Las Trampas and the Church of Nuestra Senora de Guadalupe in Santa Fe illustrates the need for a categorization based upon the degree of a similar kind of value. Las Trampas, of the greater value, has probably already undergone as much restoration as is desirable. Since Guadalupe no longer serves as a church, however, the structure can probably only be preserved if it is adapted to a new use, and therefore considerable sympathetic change is appropriate. Different criteria should apply to the two sites because they have such different

degrees of the same kind of value.

The mechanics of this proposed categorization of all sites is not complex. Top priority sites should be so labeled on the Form A. Similarly, sites which have predominantly scientific and educational value should so be labeled. Sites which fall into neither of these categories should carry no analogous label at all. The objectionable designation of second rate site would thus be avoided, as would the necessity of dividing all sites into several types.

In the case of top priority sites or sites whose values are primarily scientific and educational, no changes should be made other than stabilization and reconstruction of parts where no guess work is involved. Reconstruction should be attempted only when there is enough data regarding the rebuilt parts to eliminate any significant element of speculation. These reconstructed parts should be made clearly visible to the careful observer. Speculative reconstruction should not be attempted; restoration ceases at the point conjecture begins.

Sites of less than top priority, whose predominant values are generalized rather than specifically scientific and educational, may be extensively repaired or adapted to new uses. In these cases, reconstruction which can be adequately documented as having existed need not be visibly new. However, cases of this sort where the documentation is adequate are extremely rare. New construction should not only be clearly identifiable as new work, but ideally should be done in a contemporary but harmonious and sympathetic manner.

Total reconstruction or relocation should never be attempted except when, in the view of the Cultural Properties Review Committee, such undesirable procedures are the only means of preserving some of the values of extremely rare cultural properties.

CULTURAL PROPERTIES ON PRIVATE LAND

Excerpted from: Cultural Properties Act of the State of New Mexico, Laws of 1969, Chapter 233, Sec. 9.

A. It is the declared intent of the legislature that field archaeology on privately owned lands should be discouraged except in accordance with the provisions and spirit of the Cultural Properties Act; and persons having knowledge of the location of archaeological sites are encouraged to communicate such information to the committee.

B. It shall be deemed an act of trespass and a misdemeanor for any person to remove, injure or destroy registered cultural properties situated on private lands or controlled by a private owner without the owner's prior permission. Where the owner of a registered cultural property has submitted his acceptance in writing to the committee's registration of that cultural property, the provisions of Section 8 of the Cultural Properties Act shall apply to that registered cultural property.

C. Where a cultural property is on private land or is otherwise privately owned and the committee determines that such cultural property is worthy of preservation and inclusion on the official register, the committee may recommend the procedure best calculated to insure preservation. Such procedures may include:

1. providing technical assistance to the owner who is willing to restore, preserve and maintain the cultural property;

2. acquiring the property or an easement or other right therein by gift or purchase;

3. advising the county or municipality within which the cultural property is located on zoning the property as an historic area or district in accordance with the Historic District Act;

4. advising the county or municipality within which the cultural property is located on the use of agreements, purchases or the right of eminent domain to obtain control of the cultural property in accordance with the Historic District Act; and

5. acquiring the property for the state by use of the right of eminent domain.

BIBLIOGRAPHY

This listing of reference source material is divided roughly according to subject matter. New publications appear all the time, though some of them are obscure and hard to locate. Various Southwestern state offices of Historic Preservation can almost always be of assistance. Also, magazines such as the *Old House Journal* and *Historic Preservation* contain numerous articles of interest, though few of them are specific to adobe construction or historic Southwestern styles in particular.

HISTORIC ARCHITECTURE OF THE SOUTHWEST

Bunting, Bainbridge. *Early Architecture in New Mexico*. Albuquerque: UNM Press, 1976.
_____. *Of Earth and Timbers Made.* Albuquerque: UNM Press, 1974.
_____. "Take a Trip with NMA: An architectural guide to Northern New Mexico," *New Mexico Architecture*, Vol. 12, nos. 9, 10 (Sept.-Oct.), 1970.
_____. *Taos Adobes: Spanish Colonial and Territorial Architecture of the Taos Valley* Santa Fe: Museum of New Mexico Press, 1964 [A brief survey of historical adobe structures in and around Taos valley; illustrated with plans and elevations.]

Fergusson, Edna. "Albuquerque." Albuquerque: Merle Armitage Editions, 1947. [Reference to Whittlesey house.]

Grattan, Virginia L. *Mary Colter: Builder Upon the Red Earth.* Northland Press, Flagstaff, Az, 1980. [A pleasant and readable book about Mary Colter and her work. Miss

Colter was architect and decorator for the Harvey House, Santa Fe Railroad affiliate, executing some of the earliest and best in a genre of rustic, regional buildings at the turn of the century.]

Gritzner, Charles. "Construction Materials in a Folk Housing Tradition, Considerations Governing their Selection in New Mexico." *Pioneer America*, Vol.6, no. 1, p. 26, Jan. 1974.

Kubler, George. *The Religious Architecture of New Mexico.* Republished by the Rio Grande Press, 1962.

LaFarge, Oliver. *Santa Fe: The Autobiography of a Southwestern Town.* University of Oklahoma Press.

Loomis, Silvia Glidden, ed. *Old Santa Fe Today.* Introduction by John Gaw Meem, FAIA. School of American Research.

Miller, James M., *Glossary of Southwest Construction.* New York: Books International, 1959.

Morand, Sheila. *Santa Fe Then and Now.* Santa Fe: Sunstone Press, 1983

Sanford, Trent Elwood. *The Architecture of the Southwest.* New York: Norton Press, 1950.

Scully, Vincent. *Pueblo Architecture of the Southwest.* Fort Worth: University of Texas, 1971.

Sherman, John. *Santa Fe: A Pictorial History.* First National Bank of Santa Fe and Donning Company, 1983.

Sonnichsen, C.L. *The Southwest in Life and Literature.* New York: Devin-Adair Co., 1962.

Vierra, Carlos. "Our Native Architecture in its Relation to Santa Fe," Papers of American Archaeology, Archaeological Institute of America, No. 39, 1917.

HISTORIC PRESERVATION IN THE SOUTHWEST

Architectural Research Consultants, Inc. *Guidelines for Construction, Alteration, and Demolition within Historic Huning Highland.* City of Albuquerque Municipal Development Department - Planning Division. Albuquerque, NM. [A discussion of the historic building code in effect for the Huning Highland District of Albuquerque, with guidelines for its application and a synopsis of its general intent. Illustrated, bibliography.]

Caperton, Thomas J. *Rogue! Being an Account of the Life and High Times of Stephen W. Dorsey.* Santa Fe: Museum of New Mexico Press, 1978.

Cherry, Edith. *New Mexico Historic Building Inventory Manual.* New Mexico Historic Preservation Office and the University of New Mexico School of Architecture and Planning, unpublished, 1979.
[An expansive report surveying New Mexico's historic buildings, including procedures for dating and documenting the history of a given building.]

City Planning Department of Santa Fe. *Santa Fe*

Historic Structures and Townscape. Santa Fe, 1976.

DeWitt, Susan. *Historic Albuquerque Today: an Overview Survey of Historic Buildings and Districts. Historic Landmarks Survey of Albuquerque, NM, 1978.* [An inventory of historical buildings in Albuquerque, both existing and demolished. Includes introductory chapter on archaeological sites and collections. Illustrated, bibliography.]

New Mexico State Planning Office. *The Historic Preservation Program for New Mexico.* (David King, State Historic Planning Officer). Santa Fe: 1973. Vol. I: The Historical Background; Vol. 2: The Inventory

Planning Department of the City of Santa Fe. *Design and Preservation in Santa Fe: A Pluralistic Approach.* Santa Fe: 1973.

State Planning Office of New Mexico. *Historic Preservation A Plan for New Mexico.* Santa Fe: 1971.

HISTORIC PRESERVATION General Sources

Greiff, Constance M. *The Historic Property Owner's Handbook.* Washington D.C.: The Preservation Press, National Trust for Historic Preservation, 1977. [A property owner's guide to the legal, financial, social, technical and aesthetic responsibilities and opportunities in regard to private ownership of an historic property. Includes names and addresses of relevant agencies and funding sources.]

Grow, Lawrence. *The Old House Catalog.* New York: Universe Books, 1976. [Lists suppliers, products, services for restoration of period houses.]

Myers, John H. "The Repair of Historic Wooden Windows," *Preservation Briefs 9.* Technical Preservation Services Division, Office of Archaeology and Historic Preservation, Department of the Interior; Washington D.C.

O'Neill, John P. *Historic American Buildings Survey.* Washington D.C.: U.S. Government Printing Office, 1938.

Secretary of the Interior's Standards for Rehabilitation and Guidelines for Rehabilitating Historic Buildings. Office of Archaeology and Historic Preservation, Heritage Conservation and Recreation Service, U.S. Dept. of the Interior, 1979 [Conformance standards established by the Department of the Interior that outline and define "The General and Specific Treatments that may be applied to registered properties."

Stephen, George. *Remodeling Old Houses Without Destroying their Character.* New York: Alfred A. Knopf, 1972.

Weeks, Kay D., and David W. Look. "Exterior Paint Problems on Historic Woodwork," *Preservation Briefs 10.* Technical Preservation Services Division, Office of Archaeology and Historic Preservation, Dept. of the Interior; Washington D.C.

ADOBE

Adobe, Past and Present. Santa Fe: Museum of New Mexico Press, 1972.

Clifton, James R. "Preservation of Historic Adobe Structures: A Status Report," *National Bureau of Standards Technical Note No. 934.* Washington D.C.: Feb. 1977.

Clifton, James R., and Frankie L. Davis. "Mechanical Properties of Adobe," *National Bureau of Standards Technical Note 996.* Washington D.C.: U.S. Dept. of Commerce, May 1979.

Comey, H. Ralph, Robert C. Giebner and Albert N. Hopper. "Adobe Preservation," University of Arizona unpublished manuscript.

Crosby, Anthony. "A Preservation Monitoring System at Tumacacori National Monument," *APT Bulletin.* The Association for Preservation Technology, Vol. X, no. 2, 1978.

Doat, Patrice, et al. *Construire en Terre.* Terre-Haut Brie, France: Centre de Recherche et d'Application, 1979.

Fathy, Hassan. *Architecture for the Poor.* University of Chicago Press, 1973. [A seminal work documenting the many projects of Dr. Fathy in rural Egypt, this book outlines the basic concepts of "Appropriate Technology" as they apply to indigenous adobe architecture of Egypt. Dr. Fathy proposes a labor intensive, local material-based construction system with its roots in a long tradition of Egyptian vernacular as a solution to housing for the Arabic poor.]

Giebner, Robert. *Reading a Building: Adobe.* American Association for State and Local History, 1977.

Hopson, Rex. *Adobe: A Comprehensive Bibliography.* Santa Fe: Lightning Tree Press, 1979. [1,400 references to adobe and adobe construction.]

McHenry, Paul G. *Adobe: Build It Yourself.* Tucson: University of Arizona Press, 1973.

Miller, David J., and Lydia A. *Manual for Building a Rammed Earth Wall.* Greeley, CO: David J. and Lydia A. Miller, 1980.

O'Connor, John F. *The Adobe Book.* Ancient City Press, 1973.

"Preservation of Historic Adobe Buildings." *Preservation Briefs 5.* Technical Preservation Services Division, Office of Archaeology and Historic Preservation, Dept. of the Interior; Washington D.C.: Aug. 1978.

Rogers, Benjamin T. "Effect of Moisture Content on the Thermal Properties of Sun Dried Adobe," *Southwest Bulletin:* New Mexico Solar Energy Association, Vol. 3, no. 9, Sept. 1978, pp. 14-16.

Stedman, Myrtle. *Adobe Architecture.* Santa Fe: Sunstone Press, 1973.

Stedman, Myrtle. *Adobe Fireplaces.* Santa Fe: Sunstone Press, 1974.

Wolfskill, Lyle A., Wayne A. Dunlap and Bob M. Gallaway. *Handbook for Building Homes of Earth.* Texas Transportation Institute, Bulletin No. 21, E 14-63.

ENERGY CONSERVATION AND HISTORIC PRESERVATION
General Sources

Advisory Council on Historic Preservation. *Assessing the Energy Conservation Benefits of Historic Preservation: Methods and Examples.* Washington D.C.: January 1979. [A highly technical analysis of energy expenditures and benefits incurred through renovation/rehab in comparison to new construction. Emphasizes and documents "embodied energy" expenditures (production related). Includes 3 case studies.]

Fitch, James M., and D.P. Branch. *Primitive Architecture and Climate.* Scientific American 203:6 (134-144), December 1960.

Neblett, Nathaniel P. *Energy Conservation in Historic Homes.* Historic House Association of America. Washington D.C.: 1980.

Smith, Baird M. "Conserving Energy in Historic Buildings," *Preservation Briefs 3.* Technical Preservation Services Division, Office of Archaeology and Historic Preservation, U.S. Dept. of the Interior, Washington D.C.: April 1978.

ENERGY CONSERVATION
General Sources

ABT Associates, Inc. *In the Bank... or Up the Chimney! A Dollars and Cents Guide to Energy-Saving Home Improvements.* Office of Policy Development and Research; Division of Energy Building Technology and Standards; U.S. Dept. of Housing and Urban Development; Washington D.C.: 1977.

Derven, Ronald. *How to Cut Your Energy Bills.* Farmington, MI: Structures Publishing Co., 1976.

Dritt, James O. *Energy Conservation Code of New Mexico: Applications Manual.* New Mexico Energy Institute, Albuquerque: UNM, 1977. [The official state application manual; details energy code requirements and includes factual data in regard to building materials, climate, construction procedures, etc.]

Dumas, Lloyd. *The Conservation Response.* Lexington, MA: D.C. Heath: Lexington Books, 1976.

Ever Hear of a Retrofit! A Guide for the Home Remodeler. Washington D.C.: U.S. Dept. of Energy, October 1977.

Lee, Kaiman. *Energy Conservation and Building Codes.* Boston: Environment Design and Research Center, 1977.

Morrell, William H. *Energy Saving Handbook.* Eliot, ME: Grist Mill Publications, 1975.

Peterson, Stephen R. *Retrofitting Existing Housing for Energy Conservation: An Economic Analysis.* Washington D.C.: U.S. Dept. of Commerce, National Bureau of Standards, 1974. [A somewhat dated but nonetheless useful study outlining a "methodology for determining economically optimal levels of investment in energy conservation for reducing energy use in residential space heating and cooling." A technical report not recommended for the homeowner. Includes bibliography, heat loss methodology, climate data.]

The New Mexico Homeowner's Guide. Santa Fe: Energy Extension Service; New Mexico Energy and Minerals Department, 1978.

SOLAR ENERGY AND DESIGN

Knowles, Ralph L. *Energy and Form: An Ecological Approach to Urban Growth.* Cambridge: MIT Press, 1974. [The second chapter presents an analysis of the effective solar orientation of several Southwestern Indian settlements, including Long House at Mesa Verde, Acoma, and Pueblo Bonito.]

Stein, Richard G. *Architecture and Energy.* Garden City, NY: Anchor Press/Doubleday, 1977. [This book discusses the widely pervasive effects of energy consumption of modern planning and construction. The second chapter recaps the energy-oriented factors of traditional vernacular architecture throughout the world.]

Wessling, Francis. "Solar Retrofit Test Modules," *Southwest Bulletin:* New Mexico Solar Energy Association. Vol. 3, no. 3, June 1978, pp. 16-17.

PHOTO INDEX

MUSEUM OF NEW MEXICO PHOTO ARCHIVES

INDEX